Alliance
Academic Review
May 1999

Alliance Academic Review

May 1999

Elio Cuccaro, Ph.D.
Editor

CHRISTIAN PUBLICATIONS, INC.
CAMP HILL, PENNSYLVANIA

Christian Publications, Inc.
3825 Hartzdale Drive, Camp Hill, PA 17011
www.cpi-horizon.com

Faithful, biblical publishing since 1883

ISBN: 0-87509-863-0

99 00 01 02 03   5 4 3 2 1

Unless otherwise indicated,
Scripture taken from the HOLY BIBLE:
NEW INTERNATIONAL VERSION ®.
©1973, 1978, 1984 by the
International Bible Society.
Used by permission of
Zondervan Bible Publishers.

Scripture labeled "KJV" is taken from the Holy Bible:
King James Version.

Scripture labeled "ASV" is taken from the Holy Bible:
American Standard Version.

To Alliance academics everywhere
for their contribution
to the advancement
of Christ's kingdom

Contents

Editorial
The Stewardship of Mankind

It is a well-known principle of sound hermeneutics that the interpretation of less clear passages should be informed by the clearer relevant passages. The application of this principle to the question, "Does the Bible teach that humanity has a stewardship from God?" sends us first to the most certain and defining passages that establish and frame the biblical teaching on stewardship.

The appropriate starting point for any consideration of stewardship is the clearer and fuller revelation of the New Testament with its more abundant references. The Gospel writers record Jesus' use of the image of the steward and his stewardship in Matthew 25:14-30; Luke 12:42-48 (paralleled in Matthew 24:45-51 and Mark 13:32-37); Luke 16:1-12; and 19:11-27. Paul refers to it in First Corinthians 4:1-4; 9:17; First Thessalonians 2:4; First Timothy 1:11; and Titus 1:7. Peter relies on the image in First Peter 4:10. Other less direct references and inferences can be discerned. This New Testament information combines to say three things:

1. A steward is generally assumed to be a servant in God's household, subject to his master in all things. Thus, his subjection to the demands of the general will of his master, no matter how great, is only the expected submission and service of a servant (see Luke 17:10). As a soldier in an army is first a subject of his commander-in-chief; as an ambassador is first a citizen of the country he represents, a steward is first a servant of his master.

2. A steward is a servant entrusted with a charge (Mark 13:34) according to his ability (Matthew 25:15). This task, duty, trust or charge (generally pictured as necessitated by the master's absence) is a particular assignment above and beyond the general submission and duties of servanthood. The servant who receives this charge is thereby consti-

tuted a steward. The charge or trust given, and his administration or management of it, is his stewardship. In the New Testament, the range of possible stewardships includes managing the master's money (Matthew 25:15; Luke 19:13), caring for the master's business affairs (16:1-12), supervising the distribution of food allotments for the master's servants (12:42-48), preaching the gospel and the secret things of God (1 Corinthians 4:1; 9:17), discharging the office of elder (Titus 1:7) and ministering good to others through the use of one's spiritual gift (1 Peter 4:10). The assignment of the trust may come directly from the Master, God Himself, as in the case of Paul (Acts 9:15; 26:17-18). It may come by the appointment of the church, as in the case of the election of an elder (Titus 1:5, 7). Or it may come to light through one's personal spiritual conviction, as in the case of the Apostles' realization that they needed to focus on the ministry of the Word of God and prayer as their special trust (Acts 6:4).

3. A steward is judged with regard to the administration and the results of his stewardship, with consequences for both his stewardship and himself. Positively, the faithful (1 Corinthians 4:2; Matthew 25:20, 23; Luke 12:42; 1 Peter 4:10), trustworthy (Luke 16:11-12; 19:17) and wise (Luke 12:42) management of one's stewardship produces positive results. This fidelity and productiveness is rewarded in two ways: by enhancing one's stewardship in the Master's kingdom (Matthew 25:21, 23; Luke 12:44; 16:10; 19:17, 19) and by consigning the steward to the blessing and joy of fellowship with his Lord (Matthew 25:21, 23). Negatively, the wicked, lazy and fearful (Matthew 25:25-26); the unjust and self-serving (Luke 16:1); and the arrogant, rebellious, willful and ignorant (Luke 12:45-48) administration of one's stewardship leads to stewardship failure and loss for the Master's interests. This faithlessness and harm is punished in three ways: by depriving the culprit of his stewardship (Matthew 25:28; Luke 19:24), by inflicting temporal punishment (Luke 12:47-48) and by consigning him to eternal separation and destruction (Matthew 25:30; Luke 12:46).

Thus the New Testament picture of stewardship teaches us that the stewards of God are His servants, that is, believers, carrying out a special trust from God. This stewardship is their person-specific and highest duty in their service for God. It is the work for which they are best suited and most productive for God, if they execute it faithfully. Their efforts and results for God's cause will be especially rewarded or severely punished.

Now that we have laid out the clearer New Testament components of stewardship we can more pointedly pose the original question: "Given that the clearer and most explicit passages teach that stewardship is the province of the servants of God, does the Bible also teach that all of humanity has a stewardship from God?" The prime referent here would be Genesis 1:26, 28: "... let them rule over the fish of the sea and the birds of the air, over the livestock, over all the earth. ... Be fruitful and increase in number; fill the earth and subdue it."

Likewise, the psalmist marvels that God has given to mankind dominion over all the works of His hands (Psalm 8:6). Does not this authority to subdue and rule over all God's works entail mankind's stewardship of all the earth? Many conservationists and environmentalists operate on this assumption.

Certain factors may be cited in favor of such a universal stewardship. When Adam was placed in the Garden of Eden, he was charged with working it and taking care of it (Genesis 2:15). When the flood came, a man, Noah, was charged with rescuing all of the kinds of land animals by providing safe haven for them on the ark (chapters 6-9). Moses' law demanded consideration in the treatment of animals in such commands as, "Do not muzzle an ox while it is treading out the grain" (Deuteronomy 25:4). The idealized natural state in the vision of the kingdom of God in Isaiah 11 and 65 suggests that working toward the mutual benefit and the universal harmony of all life is most in keeping with the end to come. Therefore, all life is precious and protecting it, its ecosystems, habitats and physical environment is humanity's stewardship.

However, there is strong data that weighs against this position. The effect of Adam's sin and the curse of God in Genesis 3 broke the harmony of three relationships: man to God, man to man and man to nature. But are these relationships of equal importance? Follow redemption's story. The wicked line of Cain in Genesis 4 shows great success in the use and subduing of nature (e.g., musical instruments, domestication of animals, building cities, forging metal weapons). Seth's righteous line had its main issue in righteous men such as Enoch and Noah (Genesis 5). The righteous line wins out; all the nature worshipers perish. Next, at Sinai God gives His law, His will for humanity in two tablets: one to restore man in piety to God, the other to restore man in righteousness to men. If our concern for nature had a comparable standing, there would have been a third tablet. After all, if the restoration of man to his original harmonious relationships is in view, where is nature's tablet?

Most important in this redemptive train is the account of Romans 1. Here God's wrath is manifested against humanity. Why? Because of their ungodliness (read that to mean sinful violations of the revealed knowledge of God—violations of the first tablet). God is also judging them as inexcusable for their unrighteousness (read that to mean sinful violations of the law of God that is written upon their hearts regarding the right treatment of men—violations of the second tablet). Of one thing you can be sure, what God is really concerned about He legislates and He judges. This means that God is really, and fundamentally, concerned about two things: our relationship and conduct toward Him and our relationship and conduct toward our neighbor.

God judges in detail the stewardship of Christians, His servants. But there is not a trace of a reference about judging humanity's stewardship of nature. Nature, time, talents, resources, etc., as managed by the natural man, are ultimately weighed and counted on but two scales named Godliness and Righteousness. That is to say, when something the natural man does touches upon the glory of God in His creation or the welfare of men, only then has he triggered the radar of God's concerns.

So, then, is there a stewardship of mankind distinct from Christian stewardship? Certainly, none that can be expressed after the pattern of New Testament stewardship. Yet there remains a tangential and secondary concern here that should discourage carelessness and arrogance. A reverence for the works of God that bear His glory and for all of humanity that bears His image is certainly appropriate for both the sons of men and the sons of God.

Preface

The *Alliance Academic Review*, first issued at Council '95, is an anthology dedicated to and composed mostly by Alliance academics around the world. Comparable writing by other Alliance members is welcome. The common virtue of all writing shall be that it is consistent with and promotive of the biblical message, the ministry and the mission of The Christian and Missionary Alliance. The *Review* intends to publish, disseminate and keep in print the best work of our academic research.

To be inclusive of all theologically related disciplines, a sincere effort shall be made to accept an equal number of papers from the following five academic divisions:

1. Alliance Heritage/Church History

2. Biblical/Theological Studies

3. Church Ministries

4. Missions

5. Religion and Society/Integration of Faith and Learning

Articles submitted may have been recently published elsewhere, recently delivered orally or specifically written for the *Review*. Each is expected to be well-researched, presented and documented. The esoteric and technical should be avoided or, at least, relegated to the endnotes. *The Chicago Manual of Style*, Fourteenth Edition, is the writing style standard. It shall be the responsibility of the writer to secure copyright permission for prepublished material submitted.

Articles and correspondence should be directed to the editor:

Dr. Elio Cuccaro, Senior Editor, CPI
C/O Nyack College, Nyack, N.Y. 10960
Fax : (914) 268-5499
E-mail: Cuccaroe@nyack.edu

The authors of accepted articles will be rewarded with a modest stipend. Articles not chosen will be retained on file for possible future use, unless their return is requested.

As long as the *Review* elicits a favorable response, it will be continued as an annual series.

In This Issue

The reader will find an eclectic collection of interesting and thought-provoking articles in this fifth issue of the *Review*.

We start with an article on the Alliance distinctives by David Fessenden. He shows that the distinctives were "present truth" to A.B. Simpson, that is, historically orthodox doctrines that deserved special emphasis because they were antidotes for the errors of the day and strong remedy for people's needs. A contemporary presentation of these distinctives reminds us that they are still "present truth."

David Smith then treats us to a consideration of listening prayer: contemplative prayer that listens to God for His ministry directions. A review of the early Alliance use of such prayer highlights how important this has been to our movement.

Next, Matthew Cook takes up the issue of the Church's response to genetic engineering. He describes the various gene manipulation techniques to alert us to some very difficult decisions that we will be facing soon to remain true to the sanctity of life and the dignity of the individual.

Occupying the fourth slot, Eldon Woodcock engages us in a thorough biblical analysis of being filled with the Holy Spirit. A survey of the early Alliance teaching on this topic shows substantial fluidity in the usage of the terms describing the operations of the Holy Spirit.

In the penultimate spot is Dick Pease, a former missionary to Japan, who presents the continuing challenge of contextualization. For a missionary church, this remains a crucial subject. From his long and varied experience, Pease details and illustrates the range of positions in which the church has found itself, from cultural imperialism to syncretism.

Finally, Larry Poston discusses the impact of some of the recent trends and developments in Christian higher education—not the least of which is the changing profile of those who come to prepare for missionary service. In the last section, Larry suggests a new paradigm for Christian education that capitalizes on these changes.

Present Truths:
The Historical and Contemporary Distinctives of The Christian and Missionary Alliance

David E. Fessenden

It is safe to say that most denominations had their origin in controversy. From the medieval split between Roman Catholicism and Orthodoxy, to the rise of the various Reformation groups, to the sectarian splintering that continues to this day, it seems that every major polemic in the Church (and quite a few minor ones) has produced one or more new organizations, dedicated to promoting doctrines and/or practices that flew in the face of the prevailing religious establishment.

The Christian and Missionary Alliance is a notable exception. As one of the earliest examples of an interdenominational parachurch organization, its structure, objectives and foundational principles broke new ground. Born out of an evangelical movement that transcended denominational creeds, the society founded by A.B. Simpson sought to remain loyal to the teachings of Scripture while working within the existing churches of the time. This required that the Alliance be careful to avoid a sectarian bias or an extra-biblical slant. Simpson's goal was to produce an organization that had wide acceptance among evangelicals of all denominations and one that would tolerate differences of opinion in non-essentials. George Pardington, cited as the most influential developer of Alliance doctrine apart from Simpson,[1] put it this way:

> The doctrinal basis of the Alliance is strictly evan-
> gelical. In common with orthodox Protestantism it

unhesitatingly accepts and unequivocally teaches the fundamental truths of the Holy Scriptures. Aside from the Word of God it has no formal creed.[2]

Simpson went out of his way to stress his ties to the historic beliefs of the Church:

> First, we believe and teach all the evangelical doctrines of the Christian Church in the strictest sense; and secondly, even in what might be called distinctive teachings, we hold nothing that is not directly founded upon the Word of God. And even these are in accord with the spirit and sense of all the great standards of the Protestant churches.[3]

On the other hand, Simpson realized that in order for the movement to survive it had to be inaugurated with a distinctive vision, purpose and identity—a reason for being. Rather than appealing to the lowest common denominator in evangelicalism, he needed a set of principles and purposes that would serve as a rallying cry to the evangelical community. Simpson solved this dilemma through a distinctive *expression* of beliefs that were otherwise common to many evangelical believers at the time. What we call "Alliance distinctives" merely embody certain truths that have historical roots in many denominations. These were beliefs and practices that Simpson saw as neglected in the past but which, he was convinced, needed to be revived in this era. Pardington referred to this as the "special calling and distinctive testimony" of the young organization.

> In a word, the mission and message of the Christian and Missionary Alliance is to proclaim neglected Scripture truth and to prosecute neglected Christian work both at home and abroad:—"to give the whole Gospel to the whole world."[4]

Simpson never intended to start a denomination. Instead he envisioned "A Christian Alliance of all those in all the world who hold in unison the faith of God and the Gospel of full salvation."[5] He included, with core beliefs common to all Bible-believing Christians of his time, certain doctrines and practices that Simpson called "Present Truth."

These were theological distinctives that he believed had been neglected and that God wanted to set before the Church in this age.[6]

In this paper I will endeavor to describe these "present truths" as understood and popularized by Simpson and encapsulated in the Fourfold Gospel and the missionary imperative. Following these six sections,[7] I will highlight a few other emphases[8] that have contributed to the distinctive place of The Christian and Missionary Alliance in the contemporary Church.

The Fourfold Gospel

Throughout church history, theologians have synthesized biblical truth into simple creedal formulas and memorable catechistic statements that are accessible to the common man. Such a practice is good and proper, for it prevents theology from degenerating into an esoteric exercise among an academic elite. From the early Church's doctrine of the Trinity, to the ancient creeds, to Aquinas' Five Ways, to the Reformation watchwords of *sola Scriptura, sola gratia, sola fide,* to the various catechisms, and even to the contemporary witnessing tool "The Four Spiritual Laws," the drive has been to formulate theology into "sound bites"—long before modern politicians created the term!

It is therefore in keeping with historical precedent that A.B. Simpson developed the Fourfold Gospel[9] as the cornerstone of The Christian and Missionary Alliance. What made it distinctive, however, was his expression of a Christology that tied itself inextricably to the gospel, the central message of the Church. In this way Simpson sought to follow Paul's example to preach Christ (1 Corinthians 1:23; 2 Corinthians 4:5). His Christocentric formulation of the gospel reflected Paul's understanding of what was of "first importance" in Christianity (1 Corinthians 15:1-8).

While the Reformers had their own Christological "sound bite" of Prophet, Priest and King, it emphasized Christ's manifold ministry (the fulfillment of all human service to be given to God), not the Church's responsibility to proclaim that ministry, nor the individual believer's part in that ministry.[10] Simpson's formula placed the emphasis on Christ, but also stressed the benefits to the individual believer from a relationship with Him (Christ *Our* Savior, *Our* Sanctifier, *Our* Healer and *Our* Coming King). Moreover, the use of the term "gospel" implies the necessity to proclaim it as the Church's primary message, while the four "folds" of the phrase outline the content of the message.

The Fourfold Gospel was a healthy antidote to the many threats of a "Christless" Christianity at the end of the nineteenth century. This

Christocentric gospel repelled the traditionalism and institutionalism that were beginning to affect the Reformation churches. It also deflected the subjectivism and self-absorption inherent in portions of the medieval mystic tradition. Further, it countered the experience-based extremism of many early Pentecostals, the neo-scholastic tendencies of the Princeton theologians and the rigid doctrinal construct of the fundamentalist movement. Simpson's formula kept the focus on Christ, not on tradition, scholarship or experience, while at the same time it avoided becoming polemical. The Alliance could therefore draw from all these wells without drowning in the excesses of any of them.

The need for the Fourfold Gospel can be seen in the religious milieu of the time. All four aspects were popular, but also under attack.[11] On the one hand, Simpson's formula firmly witnessed for truth in the midst of the many voices speaking against these doctrines: modernism was rejecting Christ as a Savior from sin; B.B. Warfield and other ultra-Calvinists were casting doubt upon Christ as a Sanctifier subsequent to conversion and as a supernatural Healer for today; postmillennialists and amillennialists were denying the imminent coming of Christ to rule and reign. But on the other hand, the Fourfold Gospel served as a tempering influence to supporters of these doctrines: its Christ-centeredness was a voice of depth to the sometimes shallow "sawdust-trail" soteriology of fundamentalism; it was a voice of reason to the experience orientation of Pentecostalism; it was a voice of integrity to the opportunistic "faith healers" like John Alexander Dowie; it was a voice of balance to the extremism of some adventists.

The need to proclaim the Fourfold Gospel is evident in our day as well. While the formula and much of its accompanying terminology (such as "full gospel" and "whole gospel") has been adopted in various permutations by several other groups,[12] not all of them have been as Christ-centered as Simpson. An example of the contemporary danger of a less-than-Christocentric gospel is seen in an article in a recent "visitor's edition" of the national magazine for the Assemblies of God. In describing the distinctive doctrines of the Assemblies, this statement is included:

> Sanctification is an act of separation from that which is evil, and of dedication to God (Romans 12:1, 2; 1 Thessalonians 5:23; Hebrews 3:12). Scriptures teach a life of "holiness without which no man shall see the Lord" (Hebrews 12:14).[13]

4

Such a description is certainly incomplete in that it places the onus solely on the *believer* to become holy![14] But Simpson taught that *Christ* is the Sanctifier. While this does not mean that the believer plays *no* part in sanctification, neither is it a "pull yourself up by the bootstraps" theology.

To be entirely fair, many (if not most) Assemblies of God members would reject the idea that sanctification is anything other than a work of God's grace in the life of the believer. But from my limited experience in the Assemblies of God, I have to say that a practical and functional understanding of the active and present ministry of Christ as Sanctifier is decidedly lacking.

This tendency to disregard sanctification has not gone unnoticed, even by those within the movement. Pentecostal theologian Donald Gee called the situation "most deplorable." He traced it back to early Pentecostals who substituted the Baptism of the Holy Spirit for sanctification in their own version of the Fourfold Gospel. Gee even proposed that sanctification be included in a "fivefold gospel."[15] Indeed, the term "Fivefold Gospel" is commonly used by Pentecostal theologians today.[16]

Christ Our Savior

The first "fold" is the message of Christ as our Savior from sin. "The primary message of the Alliance is the primary message of the Gospel, and that is to the sinner," Pardington wrote. "We believe that man is a sinner, that the sinner is lost, and that there is no other name given under heaven and among men whereby a lost sinner can be saved but the Name of Jesus."[17]

As a corollary, the overriding purpose of the church is evangelism. "Every Alliance Branch [an early term for an Alliance congregation], like every evangelical church, should be first and foremost a life-saving station for the salvation of souls."[18]

Surely such a doctrinal stance, with its roots in the Reformation and in the revivalism of the early nineteenth century, would be greeted with overwhelming approval by the evangelical church of Simpson's day. But, as David Rambo points out,

> [I]n those days they didn't have clear divisions of Christendom as we now experience them. . . . Not everyone who declared some allegiance to the Word of God believed in the absolute, irreplaceable necessity

of the truth, "ye must be born again." There were fol-
lowers of Horace Bushnell who believed that young
people should grow up to consider themselves Christian and never to think otherwise.[19]

Bushnell and others espoused a theology that tied Christianity to
Western culture and watered it down to a kind of religious socialization.
One of his books, for example, "took a backhanded slap at revivalism by
arguing for long-range education as the surest foundation for Christian
experience."[20] The result was a kind of militant nominalism, as African
theologian Tite Tienou defines the term:

Nominalism refers to Christians whose Christianity
does not go beyond mere identification with a church
or religious body. Such Christians may participate in
many Christian functions of their choosing but they
want a religion that is not too demanding.[21]

Labeling Bushnell a nominalist may seem harsh, but apparently it is
shared by Mark Noll. He considers Bushnell to be a predecessor of the
modernism of the early twentieth century.

Bushnell's extensive moderation of traditional Calvin-
ism met the desires of many of his contemporaries.
They were optimistic about American democracy,
skeptical about the "vulgarity" of revivalism, anxious
for a more refined life, and eager to be intellectually re-
spectable in European eyes. Bushnell did not completely forsake his theological heritage, but he made
the way easier for others who later would.[22]

Such a "new religious orientation" fit hand-in-glove with the "social
gospel" of Walter Rauschenbusch, a contemporary of Simpson and a fel-
low New Yorker.[23] Though both Rauschenbusch and Bushnell testified
to having a seemingly traditional conversion experience,[24] they later
de-emphasized the new birth and equated salvation with socialization
into the Christian community.

Simpson's traditional Protestant heritage had not left him naive
about the dangers of a laissez-faire attitude toward a true salvation experience.

A.B. Simpson came out of a traditional protestant church. He was concerned at the many nominal believers in his day. Simpson opposed the widespread practice of receiving people who had no personal encounter with Christ and evidenced none of the fruits of salvation into church membership. His evangelistic efforts were designed to confront church members as well as non-church people with the claims of the gospel.[25]

Simpson's distinctive teaching of Christ as Savior was a defense to these challenges and a continuation of the evangelistic movement that Pardington traced back to Finney.[26]

Oddly enough, Simpson found little support from some who might have been expected to applaud his stand for salvation through Christ. The budding modernism movement, though it drew the wrong conclusions, may have had some valid criticisms of revivalism. Even among those who refused the "moderation" of the gospel by Bushnell and the reinterpretation of the gospel by Rauschenbusch, there was a nominalism of sorts. John Sawin notes that in Simpson's time "too many Christians, churches, and Christian denominations had narrowed God's salvation to only an escape from hell."[27]

The Alliance stood against such a cheapening of the miracle of new birth. It emphasized the comprehensive change that regeneration brings into a life.

> The Alliance believes . . . that "the moment a sinner accepts this Gospel, his sins are forgiven, his soul is regenerated, he becomes a child of God, and an heir of glory, and has 'access by faith into the grace wherein we stand,' and all the rights and privileges of the family of God."[28]

Simpson said of the experience of salvation:

> It is not at all a little thing. We sometimes hear that certain Christians are *only* justified. It is a mighty thing to be justified. It is a glorious thing to be born again. Christ said it was greater to have one's name written in heaven than to be able to cast out devils.[29]

The most controversial part of Simpson's soteriology (in practice, at least) was his belief that the proclamation of the gospel was "to all peoples," in obedience to the Lord's final command to "make disciples of all nations" (Matthew 28:19). It was the source of the first real friction between this visionary and his upper-class New York church when the presbytery refused to accept into membership 100 converts from the Italian quarter.[30] It was the reason for his non-segregationist policy during evangelistic meetings and his close association with black evangelist Dr. Charles S. Morris.[31] And it was a driving force behind his missionary vision.

Simpson's doctrine of salvation assumed the utter impossibility of salvation without Christ, the exclusivity of salvation in Christ, the sufficiency of salvation through Christ and the complete availability of salvation to all who come to Christ. These truths were under attack in Simpson's day as well as our own, and he was "a voice crying in the wilderness" to his generation.

The need for this distinctive teaching today is evident in the increasing promotion of an extra-Christological salvation (or "implicit faith") as expressed by Clark Pinnock and others.[32] The Alliance position is firm that explicit faith in Christ is the *only* way of salvation.

The Alliance's Christocentric position is also needed today because of its emphasis on the *completeness* and *comprehensiveness* of salvation through Christ. Though he believed that God had much more in store for believers beyond salvation, Simpson was quick to add that the Bible speaks of the Christian as a "new creation" (2 Corinthians 5:17). Salvation for Simpson was the portal into an entirely new realm of existence, the seed from which all the blessings of the Fourfold Gospel grew, and a transformation that was revolutionary, fundamental and indescribable.

> What this uttermost salvation means none of us has fully fathomed. It reaches down to the lowest depths of unworthiness, helplessness and misery. It reaches out to the widest range of sinful men and the farthest circle of human experience and spiritual need. It reaches on to the remotest age of eternity, and it will not have been fully interpreted until the Millennium shall have ended and the ages of glory begun to roll. It reaches to our temporal affairs, to our physical needs, to the outermost extremity of our being, and the innermost need of our heart and life. It is an infinite, everlasting, com-

8

plete salvation of spirit, soul and body for all time and all eternity. Blessed be His holy name![33]

Simpson, of course, held to the doctrine of substitutionary atonement: "Our sins were on Him and in Him have been put away, judicially dealt with, visited with the penalty we should have borne, the shame and suffering which we deserved."[34] His concept of the atonement, however, went beyond mere substitution to *union* with Christ: "Entering into union with Him by trusting Him and taking Him for our Savior saves us from the judgment we deserve."[35] Salvation is not just an escape from hell, but the entrance into a new relationship where all God's riches are available to us "in Christ." We share His righteous standing before God, His acceptance by the Father, His relationship with the Father and all other benefits as sons of God: "We inherit all things in Christ."[36]

Perhaps if more Christians experienced this "uttermost" salvation, there would be less need for counseling after salvation. Perhaps a key to a true revival in our day is a return to the all-sufficiency of Christ!

> Once 'twas painful trying,
> Now 'tis perfect trust;
> Once a half-salvation,
> Now the uttermost![37]

Christ Our Sanctifier

It is no contradiction that Simpson extolled the glories of salvation, yet believed in something more. "To be saved eternally is cause for eternal joy; but the soul must also enter into sanctification."[38] He compared salvation and sanctification to the difference between building a beautiful house and having the owner come and dwell in it.[39] This is probably the most succinct description of the Alliance doctrine of Christ as Sanctifier in Simpson's writings.

Sanctification is received, Simpson added, in a moment as distinct as salvation.

> This comes to us not as an evolution, but as a revolution. It comes not as a slow development and gradual growth, but as a definite crisis, clear-cut and immediate as the crossing of the Jordan by the children of Is-

9

rael and their heaping of stones in the midst of the river as a memorial that something has come to pass that could never be forgotten, something has been done that can never be undone.[40]

This crisis is marked, it is held, by the reception of the person of the Holy Ghost who brings Christ to indwell and possess the heart and life. And the only condition of receiving the Holy Spirit is a step of complete surrender and an act of appropriating faith. After this crisis experience sanctification is, we believe, gradual in the sense of the development and full maturity of the life "hid with Christ in God."[41]

The deeper life "is not a finished, crystallized condition which requires no further development or nourishment," Simpson contended, "but is simply a new beginning on a higher plane that needs to be maintained by continuous dependence upon the grace of Christ."[42]

By identifying both a crisis and a progressive phase in sanctification, the Alliance placed itself right in the center of a theological battle zone. On the one side were the "eradicationists," who maintained that the sinful nature could be "expurgated" from the believer "by a second definite work of grace."[43] This position usually resulted in a belief in some form of "sinless perfection." On the other side were the "suppressionists," who "held that the carnal nature was not eradicated but . . . needed to be suppressed by walking after the Spirit."[44] This position became associated with dispensationalism and usually negated a second work of grace.

Simpson's belief in both the crisis and process aspects of sanctification struck a balance between these theological positions. But he was not seeking some vague middle ground for the sake of peace, nor was he trying to synthesize opposite views in a Hegelian dialectic. He was simply remaining faithful to the full counsel of Scripture, which identifies a twofold sanctification process throughout its pages.

Among the "crisis" examples in Scripture, Simpson pointed to Jacob at Peniel in Genesis 32: "In that night of agony and prayer, which has become the type of many a spiritual crisis since, [Jacob] at length dies to his own sufficiency, sinks under the touch of God's withering hand, and rises into the victory of self-renunciation and triumphant faith. . . ."[45] And yet, Simpson added, the crisis at Peniel "was only the beginning of his consecrated life, for in the following chapter we find him still holding back from the fullness of God's will."[46]

By the time of the 1885 International Conference for Holiness and Healing, the two factions had become so polarized that suppressionist leaders were calling the higher Christian life an "ancient heresy."[47] Their differences seemed irreconcilable.

Simpson attended this conference, where "a number of divergent views of sanctification were expressed."[48] After listening attentively to the other speakers, "Simpson . . . asked for a special privilege and preached an impromptu sermon which has come to be known by the title 'Himself.' He emphasized that the Christian's need was not blessing, healing or sanctification but Christ Himself."[49]

This message reflected the consistently Christocentric flavor of Simpson's theology. For him, sanctification was an outworking of "Christ in you, the hope of glory" (Colossians 1:27) and "that Christ may dwell in your hearts through faith" (Ephesians 3:17). The concept of the indwelling Christ provided the divine means of the Alliance understanding of holiness. The pride and self-delusion of eradicationism, as well as the legalism and self-dependence of suppressionism, are swept away in a dynamic relationship with the living Lord.

> This [sanctified life] is not sinless perfection, nor the glorifying of our righteousness and our attainments as though we ourselves were infallible or faultless. We continue to recognize our utter worthlessness and helplessness and our entire dependence on Him alone for all that is pure, holy and useful in our lives, and our constant testimony is "I have been crucified with Christ and I no longer live, but Christ lives in me. The life I live in the body, I live by faith in the Son of God, who loved me and gave himself for me" (Galatians 2:20).[50]

The Christocentric and Christ-indwelling theology of Simpson led to a strong emphasis on dying to self: "Self dishonors God and sets up a rival on His throne."[51] If Christ is to dwell in our hearts, the ancient

11

usurper to the throne—self—must be dethroned and put to death, so that the true King can take His rightful place. "Christ lives in me" (Galatians 2:20), Simpson said, "is the offering of Isaac, the deliverance from self and even the substitution of Christ Himself for the new self."

A Christocentric slant has made it easier for the Alliance to discern between the good and the bad in new spiritual movements within the Church. For example, while other groups were caught off guard by the issue of tongues around the turn of the century (and consequently responded to it negatively, even unbiblically), the Alliance was able to be cautiously positive, stressing only that the gift must not be exalted above the Giver (a stance which eventually crystallized into the phrase "seek not, forbid not"[52]). Occurrances such as the Pentecostal movement, the charismatic renewal and, most recently, the "holy laughter" phenomena need not be rejected out of hand, accepted uncritically or interminably scrutinized for error. They can simply be measured against the ultimate standard: Christ Himself. In his teaching on trying the spirits, A.W. Tozer warned that one "giveaway" of a false experience is that "Christ is not central: He is not all and in all."[53]

Christ Our Healer

The third "fold" in the Fourfold Gospel is the doctrine of Christ Our Healer, the belief that Christ has provided for the needs of our bodies as well as our souls. Not only did Simpson believe that God was willing to heal specific illnesses, he also contended that Christ was able to "quicken [our] mortal bodies" (Romans 8:11, KJV), infusing them with the life of Christ, so that the believer can perform ministry with a physical strength beyond his own. Simpson referred to this concept as *divine health*.[54]

The doctrine of Christ Our Healer is not often mentioned in the writings of Simpson and other Alliance authors without a definite qualifier, such as the following from Pardington: "[W]hile the truth of Divine Healing is made of great importance, it is held in strict subordination to the pre-eminent truths of salvation and holiness."[55] The tone of such statements borders on defensiveness, but in the light of the era's theological milieu, it is quite understandable.

This doctrine, probably the most controversial of Simpson's declarations, cost him the support of a great many leaders and groups that might otherwise have cheerfully applauded the work of the Alliance. These critics were rightly concerned about a rash of "faith healers" in their day who exalted themselves, their ministry and the doctrine to the eclipsing of all other Christian truth. It is difficult, however, to account for the opposition to the Alliance doctrine of healing, considering that Simpson never exploited testimonies of healing for publicity purposes (a common accusation of the movement's opponents) or placed too much importance on the doctrine. It was, if anything, the least-emphasized portion of the Fourfold Gospel.

> It is most important that [healing] should be ever held in its true place in relation to other parts of the gospel. It is not the whole gospel, or perhaps the chief part of it, but it is a part, and in its due relationship to the whole it will prove to be like the gospel itself, "the power of God . . . to every one that believeth."[56]

Simpson "never allowed this teaching to supersede the miracle of the new birth or the necessity of yielding to the Holy Spirit," the authors of *All for Jesus* noted. Still, "he was vilified and ridiculed as another quack miracle worker."[57] The attacks he endured were ironic in that he was far from the only teacher of divine healing in his day, and certainly not the first, as Keith Bailey points out.

> A number of writers have made A.B. Simpson the founder of the modern healing movement, but the facts do not sustain this position. The doctrine of healing embraced by Simpson had been preached across Europe and Britain for two decades before he took up the teaching. Books on the subject of healing were already in print and widely read before Simpson experienced physical healing. He did not introduce any new tenets to the teaching. . . . Simpson was the focal point of most of the written attacks on divine healing because he was well known and because he succeeded in bringing the doctrine of healing to public notice.[58]

In fact, Bailey has noted that, although there was a great decline in divine healing after the apostolic period, there is evidence of its practice during the Reformation and even before.[59]

The Scriptures that Simpson used to defend his belief in divine healing are legion (one of his books, *The Lord for the Body*, has 275 citations from thirty different books of the Bible[60]), but one of his favorites was James 5:14-15:

> Is any one of you sick? He should call the elders of the church to pray over him and anoint him with oil in the name of the Lord. And the prayer offered in faith will make the sick person well; the Lord will raise him up. If he has sinned, he will be forgiven.

The Holy Spirit, through the Apostle James, placed this simple and symbolic practice into the hands of local church leaders. According to Simpson, this ensured that healing would be preserved from "fanaticism and presumption," would be perpetuated through the end of time and would be within easy reach of all believers.[61] Simpson also made two other important observations about this passage:

1. *It is in the form of a command.* "Divine healing ceases to be a mere privilege. It is the divine prescription for disease, and no obedient Christian can safely ignore it."[62]

2. *The passage also deals with the issue of sin.* Although Simpson clearly does not believe that all sickness is a chastisement for one's own sin, he notes that James considers it to be one possible explanation. "There is here the suggestion that the trial has been a divine chastening and requires self-judgment, penitence and pardon. There is the blessed assurance that both pardon and healing may be claimed together in His name."[63]

Simpson considered the passage in James 5 crucially important because of its clarity of *procedure* and *promise*. The procedure is a simple one and accommodates the local church organizational structure. In addition, its call for anointing with oil—symbolic of the Holy Spirit—ties it to the Old Testament. Its promise is simple as well, giving the dual assurance of physical and spiritual healing. The entire method is an exercise in faith by both the sufferer and the Church (represented by the elders).

The church elders are to be called because they serve as representatives of the local congregation. In addition, private spiritual counsel may be necessary during a healing session; the local church, with its close personal relationships, is the proper venue for this ministry.

This was probably one of the main reasons Simpson refused, unlike his flamboyant contemporary, John Alexander Dowie, to "go on the road" with his healing ministry.[64] Simpson and Dowie knew each other, and Dowie had great respect for the Alliance founder. A.W. Tozer relates in *Wingspread* how Dowie invited Simpson to join him in a series of healing campaigns across North America—to which Simpson replied, "Dear Brother Dowie, I have four wheels on my chariot [referring, of course, to the Fourfold Gospel]. I cannot agree to neglect the other three while I devote my time to one."[65]

It is just as well that Simpson turned down such a partnership. Dowie lacked the spiritual maturity and balance of Simpson; eventually he went on to develop a "ministry" that appeared to exalt himself more than Christ.

> [Dowie] founded the Christian Catholic Church in 1896 with himself as "general overseer." In 1901, along with about 5,000 followers, he established the city of Zion in northeastern Illinois and ran it as a Puritan theocracy. That same year he proclaimed himself "Elijah, the Restorer." In 1904 he took the title of "First Apostle," which he held until a year before his death [in 1907], when he was replaced by Wilbur E. Voliva as the general overseer.[66]

Such blatant pretentiousness and self-promotion was anathema to Simpson, especially as it related to the ministry of healing. In one of his books he listed several counterfeits to true divine healing;[67] under the heading of "Extravagance" is a description that could have been written specifically for Dowie:

> There is a great deal abroad today in the name of divine healing that is most objectionable and often makes one blush to be associated with the word and the work. There are people who claim to be healers and to exercise special apostolic gifts and powers and are looked upon as "great ones." . . . All these things are most undesirable. If there be a true Scriptural ministry of healing, it ought to be [as] simple, impersonal, modest and Christlike as all the other ministries of the Gospel, to give prominence to no man or woman, to exalt Jesus only and to bring the person healed into closer personal relations with Christ through his individual faith and holy consecration.[68]

Simpson has sometimes been accused of a "radical" belief in healing; he has been cited as a forerunner of the modern faith movement. But Simpson has been misunderstood by many of today's readers, according to Paul King. The Alliance founder's position on healing was actually quite moderate and in keeping with the beliefs of other well-respected Bible teachers, such as Andrew Murray. For the true predecessor of men like Kenneth Hagin, Fred Price and Kenneth Copeland, King suggests we look to Dowie.[69]

The fearless and faithful proclamation of the Alliance doctrine of healing has never been more needed than today, when the subject has become so polarized. The unbiblical position of the modern "faith teachers" is being challenged by the equally unbiblical position of the cessationists,[70] who deny classic faith teaching and all contemporary occurrences of the miraculous—including divine healing. King's research shows that Simpson and the Alliance remain firmly on a biblical middle ground.

> Writers such as Hunt, Hanegraaff, McArthur and McConnell do expose much wrong teaching and practice in the modern charismatic and faith movements. But they also oppose positions held by classic faith and holiness leaders such as Simpson, so their conclusions must be accepted critically. On the other hand, while some contemporary faith leaders' teachings contain elements of truth, they also contain serious error. Simpson and the classic faith teachers provide a balanced theology and practice of faith.[71]

What is the "serious error" inherent in the modern faith movement, and how does Alliance theology differ? The simplest and most comprehensive answer to this question is that while Simpson and other Alliance theologians were Christocentric in their doctrine of healing, the modern faith movement is anthropocentric. This difference breeds a distinct contrast between Simpson and men like Price, Hagin and Copeland. King cites a number of areas where the contrast is most visible.

For example, says King, Price has declared that it is not God who heals, but our faith—a decidedly human-centered attitude. Simpson held just the opposite view, and even said, "Faith is hindered by what we call 'our faith.' "[72] Modern faith teachers hold that the *believer* is responsible to *develop* the "faith of God"; Simpson taught that the faith to believe Christ for healing is *imparted by God*.[73] What if one is not healed? Modern faith healers would say that it is the believer's fault—he or she did not have enough faith; Simpson recognized that "while it is generally God's will to heal all who believe, God in His sovereignty may not always grant healing," writes King.[74]

The Alliance doctrine of Christ our Healer is a welcome answer to the extremes of today. It avoids the errors of the modern faith teachers on the one hand and the cessationists on the other, who expect no miracles today.

Christ Our Coming King

"The crowning message of the Alliance is the crowning message of the Gospel," Pardington said, "and that is the return to earth of the Lord Jesus Christ."[75] He goes on to specify three pillars of the Alliance belief in Christ's return: it will be personal, premillennial and imminent. The current Alliance Statement of Faith is worded similarly: "The second coming of the Lord Jesus Christ is imminent and will be personal, visible, and premillennial."[76]

Beyond that, there was and is no official Alliance position on the details of that belief. Issues such as timetables, order of events and symbolic interpretations of end-time prophecies, while discussed, are among those areas where the Alliance follows Wesley's practice of "liberty in non-essentials."[77] Simpson himself was a model of tolerance. While he was clearly pretribulational and A.J. Gordon was posttribulational,[78] he had no qualms about inviting Gordon and others to speak at his conventions "regardless of whether they agree with me in everything or not."[79]

This tolerance in itself gave the Alliance message of Christ our coming King a distinctiveness among adventist groups. It may be hard to imagine how the return of Christ can lose its Christocentric focus, but as David Schroeder points out, by arguing over details we can "turn the blessed hope into belligerent hype."[80] Though Simpson produced four books on prophecy,[81] "for him the return of Jesus was not the subject of curious speculation, but the motive for dynamic missionary activity."[82]

At first glance, "Christ our coming King" would seem to depart from the other three "folds" in the Fourfold Gospel because its direct relationship to the daily walk of the individual believer is not as obvious. And yet Simpson presented the *personal* return of Christ as the zenith of the believer's pilgrimage and the complete fulfillment of the Fourfold Gospel. All the blessings of salvation, sanctification and divine health are merely the shadow of what is to come when Christ returns for His bride.

> It [the Second Coming] is the glorious culmination of all other parts of the gospel. We have spoken of the gospel of *salvation*, but Peter says our salvation is "ready to be revealed in the last time" [1 Peter 1:5]. . . . We have spoken of *sanctification*, but John says: "When he shall appear, we shall be like him . . . and every man that hath this hope in him purifieth himself even as he is pure" (1 John 3:2-3 [KJV]). And we have spoken of *divine healing*, but Paul says: "God hath given us the earnest of the resurrection in our bodies now" [2 Corinthians 5:5, author's paraphrase], and divine healing is but the first-springing life of which the resurrection will be the full fruition.[83]

Christ's return should inspire a hope in believers that affects our daily walk. It should put in perspective those things that discourage us and tempt us to despair, and those that tend to be magnified beyond their ultimate value. It is the final blessing of the Fourfold Gospel, though we may see it "through a glass darkly" (1 Corinthians 13:12, KJV).

Simpson's premillennial stance was a strong challenge to the postmillennial position held by many modernists of his day. Just as they had redefined salvation to mean a vaguely Christian form of socialization, the modernists also redefined the millennium:

> Modern Protestants are really expecting no other millennium and no higher manifestation of the kingdom of God on earth than that which is to come about through civilization, the spread of the Gospel and the progress of Christianity among the nations.[84]

Though not habitually a polemic writer, Simpson forcefully identified this modernist idea for what it was—nonsense! Franklin Arthur Pyles notes that Simpson considered it ridiculous that a kingdom should be inaugurated without a King: "To him it is a truism that a kingdom can only be established by, and ruled over by, an actual King."[85] Just as ridiculous to Simpson was the eschatological timetable that such a belief implies.

> If it were true that 1000 years of spiritual blessings and universal righteousness must certainly precede His personal coming, then, how irrelevant, how absurd, the command to watch for His coming as an ever impending event?[86]

The postmillennial position was a favorite of the "social gospellers" and others who had utopian ideals, because it portrayed their social and political action as advancing the kingdom.[87] But "[s]o long as our theology puts it far distant . . . we can scarcely expect to live to see that consummation" and, as Pyles notes, Simpson saw that "it destroys whatever impact that return might have on the daily Christian walk."[88] It is the *imminent* return of Christ that is an incentive to the believer to live a godly life and to work in the Lord's harvest field "as long as it is day" (John 9:4).

According to Joel Van Hoogen, Simpson was also taking a stand against an amillennial position which holds to "a spiritualized millennium. The 1,000 years are understood to be figurative of the completed present period from the resurrection of Christ to His second coming. Christ's reign in this millennium is spiritual in the lives of those newborn."[89] Van Hoogen defines amillennialism as a theological position in which a spiritualized millennium (Christ's reign in men's hearts) is followed by His literal return. It is clear from Simpson's own statements, however, that amillennialists of the early twentieth century believed in a spiritual *return*:

> There are many who apply the Lord's Coming to His personal visitation to the hearts of His people. . . . We have heard people say, "Oh, it is all very well for you to talk about the Lord's Coming, but He has come to us and we are satisfied." . . . The truth is the more intimately we have Christ in our hearts the more ardently will we long for His personal and visible return, for Christ in us is "the Hope of glory."[90]

19

In another book, Simpson attributed to Roman Catholic writers the teaching that the millennial reign of Christ began at the end of the tenth century "through his vice-regent, the Pope."[91] This may have been a form of amillennialism which retained a belief in a literal return of Christ, as Van Hoogen describes, or it may simply have been another form of postmillennialism.

Though he seems to be mistaken about the form in which amillennialism appeared in Simpson's day,[92] Van Hoogen is certainly correct about Simpson's reaction to it: "The rejection of a material, terrestrial millennium for a higher spiritual one of heart or heaven (such as amillennialism may design) was to Dr. Simpson compatible with spiritualizing the creation account or the liberalizing of Jesus into an idea with no historical reality."[93] In other words, Simpson saw it as an attempt to destroy the very foundations of Christianity.

> That is what spiritualizing does. It takes out of God's book all reality and makes everything merely a dream as vague as the fooleries of Christian Science. Thank God He is real and we are real and Christ is real and the coming glory is real, and "This same Jesus shall so come again in like manner as ye have seen Him go into heaven."[94]

As we approach the new millennium, apocalyptic expectations run high—just as they did at the beginning of the twentieth century. It is imperative that we preach a balanced, Christ-centered premillennialism to guide us through the uncharted waters ahead. Simpson's teaching on the Second Coming is a driving force in the believer's daily walk—an incentive to repentance, holiness, vigilance and patience.[95] But it also has a corporate dimension: missions.

Based on Matthew 24:14—"And this gospel of the kingdom will be preached in the whole world as a testimony to all nations, and then the end will come"—Simpson said that missions is "the Lord's own appointed way of hastening His speedy coming."[96] This is therefore the final major Alliance distinctive to be considered.

Missions

"A.B. Simpson is credited as the person to link world evangelization and the coming of Christ," former Alliance President David Rambo noted. "Missions is not an activity; it is not a thing that we do; it isn't even central to the church life. It is the *hinge of history*."[97]

Simpson perceived that this "full gospel" had the power to transcend culture and language, to overwhelm the resistance of competing religions and philosophies, to defeat the seducing influence of universalism. It is no wonder that such a message would be expressed in world evangelism, especially when coupled with the motivation to "bring back the King."

Simpson's missionary vision was so strong that, at first, his eagerness overpowered his wisdom. His first missionaries, recent graduates of the Missionary Training College, were sent out by the Gospel Tabernacle in 1884, prior to the formation of the Alliance. Lacking adequate preparation, the five men met unexpected obstacles such as hostile Portuguese traders and virulent disease; one died and three others returned home in defeat. The fifth missionary served in the Congo until 1888, then returned home and died within a year.[98]

This and other tragedies and failures caused by inadequate preparation of workers led Simpson to adopt stricter training requirements and more thorough research into the fields being targeted. Field research became a hallmark of the society. "Once the Alliance had selected a target area," write T.V. Thomas and Ken Draper, "it studied the condition, customs and needs of the people in the target area to determine a plan of evangelistic attack."[99] Much of this research centered on identifying unevangelized fields, based on Simpson's interpretation of Matthew 24:14. Long before anyone used the term "unreached people groups," Simpson was keeping detailed statistics on unevangelized peoples around the globe.[100]

Simpson realized early on that reproducing a Western-style church overseas, usually amid rigid sectarianism and elaborate organization, was a major cause of failure. He recommended that his workers practice Paul's principle of becoming "all things to all men" (1 Corinthians 9:22) and work within the culture. "If [we] can better reach China by wearing Chinese dress and living in Chinese houses, [we] give up the customs and comforts of civilization that [we] may gain some."[101]

Franklin Pyles has argued that Simpson's eschatology was in conflict with the formation of indigenous churches on the mission field because he interpreted the phrase from Matthew 24:14, "a testimony to all nations," to mean a mere *presence* of the gospel; full evangelization was to be done by converted Jews during the millennium.[102] This is nothing short of a caricature of Simpson's theology; Simpson himself appears to deny the idea of Jewish millennial evangelism when he speaks negatively of those

> ... who believe and teach that this is not a missionary age. They say that after our Lord's return, a great missionary movement is to be carried on by another people and under entirely different circumstances.[103]

Furthermore, the facts of history do not bear out Pyles' claim. Indigenous churches were already beginning to be formed within Simpson's lifetime—and he wholeheartedly approved and promoted the trend.

> Native assistants, especially, should be afforded all possible help and encouragement; as they become able, they should be allowed to bear responsibility, and the element of foreign teaching, pastoral care, and supervision be gradually withdrawn.[104]

According to Thomas and Draper, Simpson considered the job of the missionary to be a temporary step in the process of developing a permanent indigenous church: "As the church matured, the missionaries were to train local people to take their place. This released missionaries to penetrate as yet unreached communities."[105] The success of this policy is seen in the fact that national workers, an outgrowth of indigenization, grew from 1,105 in 1929 to 1,854 in 1939—and this was during the decade that followed a decision to withdraw subsidies for national workers.[106]

Simpson's missionary policy was carried to its logical conclusion by the General Council of 1927, which endorsed "self-support, self-government and self-propagation for national churches issuing from missionary work."[107] Apparently, however, this approach was too radical for many missionaries to follow. By the 1950s, a stifling paternalism had set in. The new foreign secretary, L.L. King, had to implement a wholesale reeducation of missionaries and national leaders in indigenous church principles.[108]

Though it met with some resistance, the wisdom of King's indigenization policy was evident when, in 1967, the government of Guinea ordered all missionaries out of the country for the "africanization" of the churches. Because the Alliance churches in

Guinea were already africanized and enjoyed full autonomy, the regime allowed most of the missionaries to stay.[109]

Faithful support of the churches in North America made possible the worldwide efforts of the Alliance, Simpson realized. "The home guard is as necessary as the advance guard," he contended, and the work of praying and financing the missionary enterprise is only possible when those at home are "baptized" with a vision for world evangelization.[110] In order to help the laity catch this worldwide vision, "Simpson evidently invented that unique blend of Bible conference, camp meeting, evangelistic crusade and missionary promotion meeting that came to be known as the missionary convention."[111] By conducting conventions on the national, regional and local levels, the Alliance was able to solicit regular prayer and financial support, so that missionaries on furlough could report to congregations on their work without "wasting time and resources . . . raising their own support."[112]

Today the Alliance is considered a cutting-edge missions organization for policies such as the "faith promise" method of fund-raising[113] and full missionary status for women (including equal training requirements and equal salaries). Ironically, these practices have been a part of the organization since its earliest days.

Simpson's commitment to world evangelization continues to this day in the Alliance, with one missionary for every 250 inclusive members and one of the largest missionary forces in the world—over 1,100 strong. Its continuing emphasis on contextualization, indigenization and unreached peoples reflects its founder's vision to "bring back the King."

Other Emphases

While not entirely unique, a number of other emphases in the Alliance set it apart from many other groups. Among these are the following interrelated issues:

Innovation and "Evangelical Ecumenicity": A positive attitude toward creativity in ministry—both at home and on the mission field—is a direct outgrowth of the personality of its founder. It also is one of the probable reasons for Simpson's insistence that the Alliance avoid falling into a sectarian mold. Simpson often referred to the Alliance as "undenominational," though he obviously had no qualms about working with people affiliated with a particular denomination. Simpson was a churchman, but he realized that, at least in his day, denominations were entrenched, indecisive and resistant to innovation. He modeled and advocated a cooperative spirit which one writer referred to as "evangelical ecumenicity."[114]

Balance and Tolerance: The Alliance stance on tongues ("seek not, forbid not") is an excellent example of doctrinal balance. The Alliance has been scrupulous in avoiding the divisiveness and polarization that is endemic to the evangelical movement. This may explain Paul Rader and his conflicts with the rest of the Alliance leadership over the "tabernacle movement." Where Rader sought a rejection of institutionalized churches in favor of loosely organized urban tabernacles, the rest of the Alliance leadership wanted the small, mostly rural, churches to work side-by-side with the tabernacles.

The Alliance today continues to reflect doctrinal balance and tolerance in many areas, contributing to its unique flavor among evangelical denominations. (I participated in a local church membership class, for example, where newcomers to the Alliance expressed surprise—even shock!—that the statement of faith takes no position on the Calvinist/Arminean debate.) This cooperative spirit could be the way out of current controversies over worship styles and evangelism methods. Rather than either-or, why not both-and?

Simplicity in Organization, Adaptability in Structure: The Alliance began as a parachurch organization with a simple organizational structure. Because simplicity in organization allowed for flexibility and innovation, but also because he wanted to avoid any hint of sectarianism, Simpson had a decided ambivalence toward church-like structure. "He sought to provide a fellowship only," A.W. Tozer observed, "and looked with suspicion upon anything like rigid organization."[115] But as the years went by, the Alliance realized its role "would become more and more restricted unless it took on regular ministries of a church," Stoesz notes.[116] Eventually this interdenominational "fraternal society" became a denomination in 1974.

Ironically, it could be argued that the Alliance's structural adaptability has created a problematic lack of precedent. With its relatively short history and its lack of roots in any one tradition (due to its nondenominational beginnings), the Alliance finds itself struggling repetitively with issues involving church polity, such as the scope of elder authority and the ordination of women. Had the organization determined to become a denomination earlier in its history, perhaps these questions would not even be under discussion. On the contrary, they have been recurring topics at Annual Council for at least forty years!

24

However, what the Alliance might have gained in solidifying its structure and establishing precedent in church polity, it may have lost in innovation and responsiveness. It is imperative that the Alliance retain a structure capable of reacting quickly and creatively to cultural, political and societal changes, both at home and abroad.

Education and Lay Involvement: The Alliance has long been able to strike a balance between placing a high value on education and yet not limiting ministry to professional clergy. Simpson was an early pioneer in the Bible college movement, which was a reaction to an over-emphasis on secular, classical subjects in seminary training, at the expense of practical and biblical content. However, Simpson soon discovered the necessity of offering a more academically challenging curriculum to better prepare his students for ministry in the modern world.[117]

Today the Alliance boasts five colleges and two seminaries in North America and over fifty schools overseas for the training of pastors and lay persons. In addition, the denomination is an international leader in Theological Education by Extension (TEE).

Conclusion

As this great movement, which has only recently accepted a denominational identity, faces the known and unknown challenges of a new millennium, it is natural and logical that we return to our roots for perspective, inspiration and wisdom. The historical distinctives we have reviewed in this paper have served the Alliance well in the past. They will continue to do so, as we apply and adapt them with discernment in anticipation of His soon return.

Endnotes

[1] Robert L. Niklaus, John S. Sawin and Samuel J. Stoesz, *All for Jesus* (Camp Hill, PA: Christian Publications, Inc., 1986), 270.

[2] George P. Pardington, *Twenty-Five Wonderful Years, 1889-1914: A Popular Sketch of the Christian and Missionary Alliance* (New York: Christian Alliance Publishing Company, 1914), 47.

[3] A.B. Simpson, article in *The Word, the Work and the World*, July 1887, 2.

[4] Pardington, *Twenty-Five Wonderful Years*, 49.

[5] Niklaus, Sawin and Stoesz, *All for Jesus*, 64.

[6] Ibid., 74-75. Some have equated Simpson's belief in "Present Truth" with the Pentecostal doctrine of "progressive recovery" of biblical truth. Simpson, however, defines "Present Truth" in this way: "While all inspired truth is necessary and important yet

there are certain truths which God emphasizes at certain times" (*Present Truths*, 9), for the purpose of meeting the needs of the times and countering the errors of the times.

The distinction between *emphasis* and *progressive restoration* is subtle but crucial. Simpson did not see himself in the role of a "restorer," uniquely recovering teachings that had been carefully neglected for centuries. If he had, he would probably have favored the creation of a new denomination rather than a non-denominational movement—after all, if what was taught in the Alliance was "new" doctrine, it would have required "new wineskins." (This was certainly the mentality of the early Pentecostals who founded a startling number of new groups with widely varying beliefs.) Instead, Simpson sensed a calling to especially emphasize those teachings that had contemporary or historical precedent but provided strong remedy for the errors and needs of the times. While at least one passage in Simpson's writings indicates his belief in a post-Reformation "unfolding" of neglected truths (see *The Word, the Work and the World*, May 1882, page 148), the context indicates a normal historical development of theology and has no connection to his concept of "Present Truths."

[7]   In addition to a section on the Fourfold Gospel, each "fold" (Christ as Savior, Sanctifier, Healer and Coming King) is presented in a separate section, followed by a section on missions, for a total of six. It should not be seen as redundant that the Fourfold Gospel is presented separately from each of its "folds." The Fourfold Gospel, as a comprehensive concept, was one of Simpson's unique innovations.

[8]   In this paper, the term "distinctive" is used for those major doctrinal and practical articles that are to some degree unique to The Christian and Missionary Alliance (at least in expression). The term "emphasis" is used for articles not unique to the Alliance but which nevertheless contribute to its individual denominational culture.

[9]   The term itself has a rather mysterious origin, though his contemporaries generally attributed it to Simpson. The Alliance founder's first use of the phrase has never been discovered. In 1882 Simpson described the content without the term while writing about Luther and the Reformation; in 1883 he published an article on salvation and healing which he entitled "The Twofold Gospel"; by 1887 he was using the term in his magazine as if it were commonly understood (see articles by Simpson in *The Word, the Work and the World*, May 1882, p. 148; April 1883, p. 61; and March 1887, p. 192, respectively). All this would seem to indicate that the term evolved over a period of time. On the other hand, on page 36 of *Sanctification: An Alliance Distinctive* (Camp Hill, PA: Christian Publications, Inc., 1992), author Samuel J. Stoesz attributes the origin of the first three "folds" of the Fourfold Gospel to W.E. Boardman.

[10]   John Calvin, *Institutes of the Christian Religion*, bk. 2, ch. 15, sec. 1. Though later sections speak of the benefits believers derive from these offices, the "sound bite" itself speaks only of Christ's offices.

[11]   Niklaus, Sawin and Stoesz, *All for Jesus*, 74-75.

[12]   Samuel J. Stoesz, *Understanding My Church: A Profile of The Christian and Missionary Alliance* (Camp Hill, PA: Christian Publications, Inc., 1968, 1983), 135.

[13]   "What We Believe," *Pentecostal Evangel*, Feb. 15, 1998, 10.

[14]   Ironically, the statement cites First Thessalonians 5:23, which attributes the work of sanctification to God alone.

[15]   Donald Gee, *Now that You've Been Baptized in the Spirit* (Springfield, MO: Gospel Publishing House, 1972), 55.

16 For example, "The Fivefold Gospel" was the theme of the 1997 annual meeting of the Society for Pentecostal Studies (*SPS Newsletter*, Vol. XXVII, No. 1 [May 1997]).

17 Pardington, *Twenty-Five Wonderful Years*, 50.

18 Ibid., 53.

19 David Rambo, *Our Hope for the Future* (Camp Hill, PA: Christian Publications, Inc., 1996), 4.

20 Mark A. Noll in *Who's Who in Christian History*, ed. J.D. Douglas, Philip W. Comfort and Donald Mitchell (Wheaton, IL: Tyndale House, 1992), 120.

21 Tite Tienou, as quoted by Arnold Cook in *Why Be Missionary?* (Camp Hill, PA: Christian Publications, Inc., 1996), 10.

22 Noll, *Who's Who in Christian History*, 120.

23 Daniel J. Evearitt in *Alliance Academic Review 1997*, ed. Elio Cuccaro (Camp Hill, PA: Christian Publications, Inc., 1997), 1.

24 Ibid., 2; Noll, *Who's Who in Christian History*, 120.

25 Keith Bailey, *Bringing Back the King* (Colorado Springs, CO: The Christian and Missionary Alliance, 1985, 1992), 93.

26 Pardington, *Twenty-Five Wonderful Years*, 14.

27 John Sawin in *Birth of a Vision* (Camp Hill, PA: Christian Publications, Inc., 1986), 7.

28 Pardington, *Twenty-Five Wonderful Years*, 51-52. The source of the quoted material in this passage is not identified.

29 A.B. Simpson, *The Fourfold Gospel* (Camp Hill, PA: Christian Publications, Inc., 1984), 11.

30 Niklaus, Sawin and Stoesz, *All for Jesus*, 36.

31 Ibid., 169-170.

32 See K. Neill Foster, "Implicit Christians: An Evangelical Appraisal," in *Alliance Academic Review 1998*, ed. Elio Cuccaro (Camp Hill, PA: Christian Publications, Inc., 1998), 123-146.

33 A.B. Simpson, *The Christ in the Bible Commentary*, vol. 6 (Camp Hill, PA: Christian Publications, Inc., 1994), 118.

34 A.B. Simpson, *Christ in You* (Camp Hill, PA: Christian Publications, Inc., 1997), 24.

35 Ibid.

36 Ibid., 24-27.

37 A.B. Simpson, "Himself" (poem), in *Wholly Sanctified* (Camp Hill, PA: Christian Publications, Inc., 1991), 120.

38 Simpson, *Fourfold Gospel*, 24-25.

39 Ibid., 25.

40 A.B. Simpson, *Christ Our Sanctifier* (Camp Hill, PA: Christian Publications, Inc., 1996), 15.

41 Pardington, *Twenty-Five Wonderful Years*, 54.

42 Simpson, *Christ Our Sanctifier*, 13.

43 Samuel J. Stoesz in *The Birth of a Vision*, 114.

44 Ibid., 115.

45 A.B. Simpson, *The Christ in the Bible Commentary*, vol. 1 (Camp Hill, PA: Christian Publications, Inc., 1992), 83.

46 Ibid., 84.

47 Samuel J. Stoesz, *Sanctification: An Alliance Distinctive* (Camp Hill, PA: Christian Publications, Inc., 1992), 47.

48 Stoesz in *Birth of a Vision*, 114.

49 Ibid., 116.

50 Simpson, *Christ Our Sanctifier*, 12.

51 A.B. Simpson, *A Larger Christian Life* (Camp Hill, PA: Christian Publications, Inc., 1988), 77.

52 *The Gift of Tongues* (Colorado Springs, CO: U.S. National Office of The Christian and Missionary Alliance, n.d.).

53 A.W. Tozer, *Man: The Dwelling Place of God* (Harrisburg, PA: Christian Publications, Inc., 1966), 124.

54 A.B. Simpson, *The Lord for the Body* (Camp Hill, PA: Christian Publications, Inc., 1996), 9.

55 Pardington, *Twenty-Five Wonderful Years*, 57.

56 A.B. Simpson, *The Gospel of Healing* (Camp Hill, PA: Christian Publications, Inc., 1994), 6.

57 Niklaus, Sawin and Stoesz, *All for Jesus*, 42.

58 Keith Bailey, *Divine Healing: The Children's Bread* (Camp Hill, PA: Christian Publications, Inc., 1977), 227.

59 Ibid., 211 ff.

60 Simpson, *The Lord for the Body*, 143-147.

61 Simpson, *Gospel of Healing*, 17.

62 Ibid., 19.

63 Ibid.

64 N.V. Hope in *Who's Who in Christian History*, 242.

65 A.W. Tozer, *Wingspread* (Harrisburg, PA: Christian Publications, Inc., 1943), 135.

66 Ibid.

67 A.B. Simpson, *The Old Faith and the New Gospels* (Harrisburg, PA: Christian Publications, Inc., 1966), 60-66. The counterfeits listed include Roman Catholic miracles, spiritism, extravagance, Christian Science and Emmanuelism.

68 Simpson, *The Old Faith and the New Gospels*, 61.

69 Paul King in *Alliance Academic Review 1996*, ed. Elio Cuccaro (Camp Hill, PA: Christian Publications, Inc., 1996), 11.

70 *"Cessationist* refers to someone who thinks that certain miraculous gifts *ceased* long ago, when the apostles died and Scripture was complete." Wayne Grudem, *Systematic Theology* (Grand Rapids, MI: Zondervan, 1994), 1031.

71 Paul King in *Alliance Academic Review 1996*, 13.

72 Ibid., 7-8.

73 Ibid., 8-9.

74 Ibid., 10

75 Pardington, *Twenty-Five Wonderful Years*, 61.

76 Bailey, *Bringing Back the King*, 83.

77 A March 1906 announcement of a conference on Alliance testimony and teaching (held in May 1906) included this statement on the Lord's return: "Liberty is accorded to our teachers in connection with the various opinions about Anti-Christ, the Tribulation, the Last Week of Daniel, Rapture, etc., but with the understanding that any spirit of antagonism and strife toward those who may hold different opinions is discountenanced." Though the minutes of the conference are lost, that statement was apparently ratified and remains in effect. See Sawin in *Birth of a Vision*, 23-24.

78 Franklin Arthur Pyles in *The Birth of a Vision*, 30-31. It should be noted, however, that *Bringing Back the King*, a book published by the Office of Alternative Education to teach Alliance history and thought, is overtly pretribulational.

79 Niklaus, Sawin and Stoesz, *All for Jesus*, 82. Gordon did speak at the Gospel Tabernacle during an October, 1891, convention (*All for Jesus*, 93).

80 David E. Schroeder, *The Centrality of Jesus Christ in the Fourfold Gospel* (Camp Hill, PA: Christian Publications, Inc., 1994), 8.

81 Pyles in *The Birth of a Vision*, 42.

82 Schroeder, *Centrality*, 8.

83 Simpson, *The Fourfold Gospel*, 53-54.

84 Simpson, *The Old Faith and the New Gospels*, 77.

85 Pyles in *The Birth of a Vision*, 36.

86 Ibid., 37, quoting Simpson in the June 8, 1898, issue of *The Christian and Missionary Alliance*, 533.

87 Daniel J. Evearitt, *Body and Soul* (Camp Hill, PA: Christian Publications, Inc., 1994), 45.

88 Pyles in *The Birth of a Vision*, 37.

89 Joel Van Hoogen in *Alliance Academic Review 1998*, 43.

90 A.B. Simpson, *The Coming One* (New York: Christian Alliance Publishing, 1912), 10-11.

91 Simpson, *The Old Faith and the New Gospels*, 76.

92 In Van Hoogen's defense, it is quite likely that he is not mistaken but is merely giving a general definition of amillennialism, while Simpson is speaking against a specific form. In summarizing the three basic millennial positions, Van Hoogen prefaces his definitions with the following statement: "It is not possible without some significant generalizing to discuss the various eschatological positions on the millennium. There

is a wide range of interpretive variance in each of the three positions outlined" (*Alliance Academic Review 1998*, 43).

93 Ibid., 45.

94 Simpson, *The Coming One*, 15-16.

95 Ibid., 201-211.

96 Niklaus, Sawin and Stoesz, *All for Jesus*, 73.

97 Rambo, *Our Hope for the Future*, 19 (author's italics).

98 Niklaus, Sawin and Stoesz, *All for Jesus*, 59-60.

99 T.V. Thomas with Ken Draper in *Birth of a Vision*, 208.

100 Ibid.

101 Ibid., 209, quoting A.B. Simpson, *The Challenge of Missions* (New York: Christian Alliance Publishing Co., 1926), 67-68.

102 Pyles in *Birth of a Vision*, 41.

103 A.B. Simpson, *Called to Serve at Home* (Camp Hill, PA: Christian Publications, Inc., 1998), 7.

104 Thomas and Draper in *Birth of a Vision*, 211.

105 Ibid.

106 Niklaus, Sawin and Stoesz, *All for Jesus*, 190, 177.

107 Ibid., 213.

108 Ibid., 213-215.

109 Ibid., 223-224.

110 Simpson, *Called to Serve at Home*, 2ff.

111 Thomas and Draper in *Birth of a Vision*, 208.

112 Gerald E. McGraw in *Alliance Academic Review 1995*, ed. Elio Cuccaro (Camp Hill, PA: Christian Publications, Inc., 1995), 112.

113 The "faith promise" is a method in which the amount an individual gives to missions is a commitment to God and not to the church or organization. This method allows the organization to plan for a certain level of giving without the commitment becoming human-centered.

114 Samuel Stoesz, *Understanding My Church* (Camp Hill, PA: Christian Publications, 1968, 1983), 122.

115 Tozer, *Wingspread*, 103.

116 Stoesz, *Understanding My Church*, 136.

117 Jacob P. Klassen, "A.B. Simpson and the Tension in the Preparation of Missionaries," in *Birth of a Vision*, 241-259.

Listening Prayer:
Listening to God for Life and Ministry

David John Smith

Listening prayer is a form of contemplative prayer which emphasizes listening to God for Christian living and effective ministry. Listening prayer is *contemplative* because it fosters laying aside thoughts, words and emotions, and opening the mind and heart of the whole being to God who is the ultimate reality.[1] Listening prayer also goes beyond contemplative prayer and personal integration of self. It has as its goal *listening* for guidance, direction, answers and insight—often within active ministry—beyond oneself. In other words, *listening prayer is a reflective kind of prayer with a purpose to hear from the Lord for specific action.*

This paper will examine the contemplative roots in The Christian and Missionary Alliance in relation to the contemporary understanding of listening prayer. Further historical analysis of the early Alliance movement will underscore how critical listening prayer was for effective ministry. Finally, constructive analysis will propose primary issues that need to be addressed in explaining listening prayer for today.

A. A Model for Listening Prayer

The Alliance is a Protestant, evangelical denomination founded in 1887 out of two passions in ministry of its founder, Dr. Albert B. Simpson—deeper life in Christ and worldwide evangelization. Its historic roots grew from five movements prominent in the late nineteenth century: gospel evangelism, the holiness movement, the divine healing movement, the modern missionary movement and the rebirth of premillennialism.

The spirituality of the early leaders of the Alliance was influenced by the contemplative emphasis found in the seventeenth-century Quietism movement. Authors such as Madame Guyon, François Fénelon and Miguel de Molinos held the conviction that God's voice could be heard in quietness and stillness. At times, early Alliance leaders encouraged Christians to read these writings, which expressed biblical principles for cultivating spiritual disciplines for an inner life in relationship with God. They did not embrace the entire Quietism movement, but they had no difficulty in assimilating certain aspects into their spirituality while endeavoring to balance contemplation with action.

Listening prayer was like a hidden spring, nurturing and inflaming the passions of early Alliance leaders. The essence of listening prayer was particularly embedded in the writings of two primary leaders of the Alliance: founder Albert B. Simpson (1843-1919) and early Alliance scholar and theologian George P. Pardington (1866-1915). Simpson had learned and taught the contemplative power of stillness: "There is, in the deepest centre of the soul, a chamber of peace where God dwells, and where, if we will only enter in and hush every other sound, we can hear His still, small voice."[2] He wrote nearly a century ago about the frenetic pace of life and the need to slow down to listen to God:

> These days of waiting are important also that we may listen to God's voice. We are so busy that we cannot hear. We talk so much that we give Him no chance to talk to us. He wants us to hearken to what He has to say to us. He wants us on our faces before Him, that He may give us His thought, His prayer, His longing, and then lead us into His better will.[3]

Various dimensions of listening prayer can be gleaned from Simpson and Pardington which embody a *model* for listening prayer. *The following presents seven phases of listening prayer as a practical pattern.*[4]

1. Relax and Be Silent

To enter listening prayer we need to relax physically and be silent. We deliberately let go of everything—tension, worry, anxiety, frustration—and seek to relax in God's presence and to obey the command given through the psalmist, "Be still, and know that I am God" (Psalm 46:10). This can include simple techniques such as finding a quiet, private place, bringing thoughts into focus, expressing feelings to God through bodily posture and dealing with distractions.[5] Pardington gave the following instructions for a daily quiet time with God:

> Get alone each day with God at a time when there will be no intrusion; open your whole being to the free operation of the Holy Spirit; consciously and voluntarily drink in His fullness until every part of your being is filled and thrilled with His divine presence and power.[6]

External silence can foster internal silence. We recognize that "God speaks to those who keep silence."[7] Evangelicals are often guilty of ignoring the physical aspects of relaxation and silence. Pardington, however, did not.

> So if we would know the will of God and hear His voice when He speaks, we must get quiet at His feet. We must cease from ourselves and our own ways. The clamorings of our own hearts must be stilled. The wandering and opposing thoughts of our minds must be quieted. We must even get ourselves into an attitude of physical and mental repose before Him. Silence must reign throughout our soul; stillness must pervade our entire being.[8]

Simpson wrote an intriguing hymn entitled, "Breathing Out and Breathing In," with this first stanza:

> Jesus, breathe Thy Spirit on me,
> Teach me how to breathe Thee in,
> Help me pour into Thy bosom
> All my life of self and sin.
>
> I am breathing out my own life,
> That I may be filled with Thine;
> Letting go my strength and weakness,
> Breathing in Thy life divine.[9]

The rest of the hymn talks about breathing *out* the sinful nature, sorrows and longings, and breathing *in* cleansing fullness, joy and comfort, peace and rest, and answers. It is reading too much into this hymn to suggest that Simpson was endorsing breathing techniques for listening prayer. It is not, however, pressing the limits to say that Simpson connected physical breathing with spiritual cleansing and receiving. In the context of this paper, following the directives of this hymn does help create an atmosphere in which to listen to God.

The first phase in listening prayer is to physically relax and be silent. Get alone with God. Sit at Jesus' feet. Prepare to drink in the Spirit's fullness. Deliberately let go of tension, worry and frustration. Seek to relax in God's presence. Let external quietness foster internal silence.

2. Become Aware of God's Presence

In listening prayer we need to open ourselves to an awareness of God's presence, attentiveness and care. We take time to recollect that God dwells at the core of our being. We learn to practice the divine presence by acknowledging the God who is really there and by affirming that this God is with us.[10] Simpson acknowledged that following a quieting phase, there comes an awareness phase:

> God was waiting in the depths of my being to talk to me if I would only get still enough to hear His voice. ... And as I listened and slowly learned to obey and shut my ears to every sound, I found after awhile that when the other voices ceased, or I ceased to hear them, there was a still, small voice in the depths of my being that began to speak with an inexpressible tenderness, power and comfort. As I listened it became to me the voice of prayer, the voice of wisdom, and the voice of duty.[11]

After a quieting of mind and body, there comes a lifting of the soul toward heaven and an awareness that Christ is with us and in us.

The second phase in listening prayer is to become aware of God's presence. Recollect that God dwells at the core of your being. Remind yourself that Christ is in you and you are in Christ. Affirm that God is here with you now and the Holy Spirit is upon you. Lift your total being heavenward.

3. Surrender and Obey

Awareness leads into surrender. We make a conscious attempt to hand back to God all that we are, all that we possess, all that we do and all that we feel. This aspect is seen in part of a covenant that Pardington made with God to hear and obey God's voice:

> I determine and promise to obey God's voice upon every occasion and to any extent. I determine and promise to listen and hear His voice. I determine and promise to be quiet and still upon every occasion till I hear His voice. I will on no occasion do anything until I definitely and satisfactorily get God's voice in regard to it.[12]

Pardington also believed that whenever God speaks we must mind, and whatever God commands, we must implicitly obey.[13] If God is going to speak to us, we must be willing to obey what God tells us to do before we are told. Surrender to God was not a one-time occasion for him, but part of his regular spiritual discipline and ongoing promise and mind-set to listen to God in obedience.

The third phase in listening prayer is to surrender and obey. Make a conscious attempt to hand back to God all that you are, all that you possess, all that you do, all that you feel. Be willing to listen, hear and obey whatever God directs—before you are told.

4. Accept, Repent and Forgive

Acceptance, repentance and forgiveness often follow surrender. We invite God to put His finger on specific situations, sins or attitudes which block our ability to listen to Him. We welcome whatever God will communicate to us through our acceptance. Once God has put us into the divine light, our response may be to confess our sins and to receive and accept forgiveness.

With roots in the holiness movement, the Alliance positively emphasized Jesus as Sanctifier. Its leaders were particularly sensitive to confession of sin and death to the sins of the self-life. Slogans emerged in hymns written by Simpson: "I Will Say 'Yes' to Jesus," "I Want to Be Holy," and "Search Me, O God."[14] Personal holiness was perceived as preceding power for service. Anything that would prevent listening to God for effective service was to be removed.

The fourth phase in listening prayer is to accept, repent and forgive. Invite God to put His finger on specific situations, sins or attitudes which block your ability to listen. Welcome whatever God communicates. Respond willingly—accept a cross, confess sins, forgive others. Receive freely—the grace to bear, the forgiveness of sins, a love for others.

5. Enter Contemplation

Following these preparation phases of quietness and patient waiting in listening prayer, we enter a contemplative phase of gazing upon God and lingering in satisfied silence. We turn ourselves entirely to God's presence, to look at God in love, to hold the awareness of God's near presence, to linger in the presence of God, to enjoy God.

Genuine contemplative prayer was like an underground spring for early Alliance leaders. This prayer of silence enabled the believer, according to Simpson, to enter into "deep communion too sacred for speech where the heart of love sinks into the heart of God in unutterable oneness, worship, and stillness."[15] He also wrote that in contemplative prayer we come to the end of our words and enter a deepening communion with God:

> The deepest kind of prayer is often voiceless. It is communion. It does not ask for anything, but it just pours out its being in holy fellowship and silent communion with God. Sometimes it is an infinite rest to cease all our words and just lie still and rest upon His bosom. . . . There are moments too sacred, too divine for our interpretation. There are joys as well as groans which "cannot be uttered" . . . we should know the depths and heights of silent prayer and divine communion.[16]

While this may seem like standard fare in the historic Roman Catholic tradition, this dimension of contemplative prayer is least understood in Protestant traditions. Many Alliance people need to return to their roots of contemplative prayer. There are fears of eastern mysticism, religious emotionalism and blind experientialism. These fears are well founded. There is a fine line between godly listening and the perilous possibility of the occult.

Still, this understanding of rest and intimacy offered by Christ was viewed very differently from the stillness required by Buddha.[17] Alliance leaders clearly distanced themselves from the Nirvana of the Buddhist which they viewed as a kind of self-annihilation. Simpson differentiated between peace *with* God which results from the atoning and justifying work of Christ and the peace *of* God which results in an inner sense of rest as the outgrowth of a deeper life with God and the holy practice of quietness and stillness.

The fifth phase in listening prayer is to enter into contemplation. Gaze upon God in love. Hold the awareness of God's near presence. Enjoy God. Commune with your living, risen and ascended Lord Jesus. Drink in the Spirit's presence and power. Linger in satisfied silence.

6. Receive Grace and Express Gratitude

Contemplation is not an end in itself but a beginning. Enjoying the afterglow of God's coming and receiving whatever benefit God chooses to extend often follows. Simpson wrote with excitement:

> The best thing about this stillness is that it gives God a chance to work . . . and when we cease from our works, God works in us; and when we cease from our thoughts, God's thoughts come into us; when we get still from our restless activity, God worketh in us both to will and do of His good pleasure, and we have but to work it out.[18]

Personal benefits of grace can include self-knowledge, fruits of the Spirit or freedom. Receiving grace results in savoring the gifts God brings and expressing gratitude to God for who He is and for what He is doing.

The sixth phase in listening prayer is to receive grace and express gratitude. Enjoy the afterglow of God's coming to you. Receive whatever benefit God chooses to extend—knowledge about yourself, fruits of the Spirit, freedom. Savor these gifts God brings. Express gratitude to God for who He is and what He is doing.

7. Listen Specifically and Move to Action

Listening prayer has as its specific goal listening for action. Internal activity leads to specific listening and external action. Essentially, we ask Paul's question, "What shall I do, Lord?" (Acts 22:10).[19] Typically, evangelicals are task-oriented. They are justifiably committed to the task of the Great Commission to make disciples of all nations. But without the preliminary dimensions of transforming listening prayer, action can become alienated from the heart of God, skewed from a biblically informed mind and centered around building a personal kingdom. Early Alliance spirituality, however, understood both sides of contemplation and action.

The seventh phase of listening prayer is to listen specifically and move to action. Listen for guidance, direction, answers and insights for your life, family and ministry. Move beyond yourself to fulfill the task God gives.

B. Practical Examples for Listening Prayer

The culmination of listening to God is effective ministry. In March of 1958 the Cistercian monk, Thomas Merton, was overwhelmed with the discovery of people as inseparable from God and from one another while he was standing in the middle of a shopping district in Kentucky. William Shannon notes that Merton's contemplative insight illustrates the need for the movement from contemplation to action.

> This experience, which was profoundly contemplative, took place not in the monastery but on a street corner in a busy city. Merton's reflections show how profoundly he came to see the responsibility of contemplatives to understand what is going on in their own times and to respond to historical needs out of a contemplative perspective.[20]

Listening prayer is not an end in itself. Listening to God has as its goal ministry to people. The contemplation of God moves us into action. Experiencing the love of God moves us toward love for people. Listening prayer moves us into ministry. We ask ourselves not only what God is saying to us personally, but what God is asking us to take from this time with God into our world: to our spouse, our children, our colleagues, our friends, our neighbors, our society, our world.[21] Listening prayer is the launching pad for effective service.

In early Alliance spirituality, intimacy with God was also inextricably linked to fruitful ministry. Deeper life in God was described in both contemplative and active dimensions. Both aspects of stillness and power were frequently used in discussions of the Spirit-filled life. Simpson himself "was a man of action whose life represents an integration of the contemplative and active dimensions of the Christian life."[22] He was aware of imbalance in either direction:

There is a subtle danger, however, for intensely spiritual minds, to carry the internal side too far and to lose the perfect balance of character which includes the active and the practical, as well as the inward and the spiritual sides of our being. Mary and Martha together form the perfect combination; sitting at the feet of Jesus, and also serving with busy ministering hands; "not slothful in business; fervent in spirit; serving the Lord."[23]

Pardington commended the quiet and seclusion found in monasticism, but equally believed that spiritual absorption could lead to the neglect of one's duty. The promise of the divine presence was for ordinary people, "not alone for the cell and the cloister, but for the office and the busy marts of trade."[24] Simpson also cautioned against a monkish way of life that isolated one from the responsibilities of practical Christian living.[25] Pardington promoted an ideal combination of both contemplative and active aspects within a Christian as the mystic-missionary, while Simpson has been described as an evangelical "Pauline mystic."[26] Listening prayer was historically the basis in the Alliance for activity in intercessory prayer, speaking to others, sermon preparation, leading services, the ministry of healing, the academic environment, public conventions, and missionary service.

1. Intercessory Prayer

Times of listening prayer can lead into intercessory prayer. In prayer we pass a person or situation into God's all-knowing, all-capable, all-caring hands, and listen for an answer to the questions, "Lord, is there anything You would like me to do for this person to show them You are in control or that You care? What can be done in this situation?"

Pardington provided instruction for intercession that flowed out of listening prayer. He taught that as believers patiently wait upon the Lord in silence, they soon become strangely sensible of a new life enkindling their whole being. Spiritual desires begin to well up in the heart. The mind becomes centered upon some subject which they may not have thought of before. They find themselves getting hold of God with a new sense of access. Longings and yearnings take possession of the heart, while words flow spontaneously from the lips in the ministry of intercession.[27]

Listening to God in prayer formed the energy, ideas and direction for the work of intercession. While stillness was considered the deepest form of prayer, intercession was viewed as the highest. Deep attentiveness to the still, small voice of the Spirit within gave direction for intercessory prayer.[28] Pardington wrote, "Meditation is the seed; communion is the blossom; and prayer is the fruit."[29]

2. Speaking to Others

Listening prayer was viewed as essential in knowing what tailor-made message needed to be spoken to another for their encouragement. Pardington felt that a believer may be ready and willing to speak God's message to someone, but may not know just what that message is. God thus awakens the believer in order to whisper heart messages into his inner ear.[30] The movement from the internal to the external was the normative order:

> God starts at the center and works outward. . . . When the heart is prepared He can reach the ear; when the ear is prepared He can reach the tongue; when the tongue is prepared He can give the message; and when the message is received He can sustain through us him that is weary.[31]

3. Sermon Preparation

Simpson's method of sermon preparation included a prayerful reception of listening prayer through hushing his spirit and ceasing to think. Then in the silence of his soul, he would listen for the still, small voice of God in order to receive messages to preach. This, of course, did not replace serious biblical and exegetical preparation, but was combined with it.[32]

4. Leading Services

Josephus Pulis was a recovered alcoholic who served as an elder in the First Alliance Church and as a member on the Board of Managers for many years. His primary ministry was to serve as assistant to the manager in the chapel of New York Christian Home for Intemperate Men. He believed that silence increased one's receptivity to the gentle ways in which God comes through instinct, intimation and intuition. It was his custom to engage in silent meditation for a half hour prior to leading daily morning and afternoon services. This method of quiet preparation would lead into a ministry of anointed power.[33]

5. The Ministry of Healing

Kenneth Mackenzie, another first-generation Alliance leader and theologian on healing, thought that divine healing was most effectively appropriated through stillness. In uniting spirit, soul and body, many physical ailments were often diagnosed as spiritual maladies, especially the lack of stillness of soul.[34]

Sarah Lindenberger played a leading role in a home for healing. She believed that a personal knowledge of God acquired through stillness was more effective in ministry than just intellectual Bible study or worked-up prayer.[35] Moreover, without the practice of stillness of soul, one's ability to work effectively for God would ultimately fade. Providing a healing home as a retreat center institutionalized stillness by providing "a quiet resting place where people could come for careful and thorough Biblical teaching in the things of the Spirit."[36] In this setting of physical quietness and rest as well as spiritual reflection and prayer, numerous people were healed.

6. The Academic Environment

The early years of the Missionary Training Institute in Nyack, New York provided the academic environment with regularly scheduled times of silence. Students were encouraged to observe a "Quiet Hour" intended for quiet meditation and prayer. Public "Quiet Hour Services" included five to ten minutes of silent prayer. These intentional structures were put in place to foster time alone with God. The geographical location itself was an ideal spot for communion with nature and with God. Nurturing spiritual vitality, mental vigor and physical well-being promoted a holistic integration for Christian life and service.[37]

7. Public Conventions

Early Alliance public conventions also incorporated a "Quiet Hour Service" which was followed by two hours of messages on the deeper life. This organizational method was based on the underlying belief that as believers spent time waiting upon God in quietness and silence, it instilled an expectation of God's presence and activity and increased a responsiveness to the preached Word of God.[38]

8. Missionary Service

Pardington wrote how waiting upon God in quietness and solitude also transformed and motivated people into missionary service:

William Carey saw God and left his shoemaker's bench and went to India. William Cassidy got a vision of God and went to China. . . . Hundreds of notable consecrated young people at our Missionary Institute have received a vision of God and today are in the uttermost parts of the earth, working for the evangelization of the heathen and the speedy coming of our Lord.[39]

The point of these extensive historical references is to underline the consistent pattern that contemplation led to action through listening prayer. The norm for early Alliance spirituality was always to precede ministry with prayerful listening to God. Ministry could not be effective without listening. Effective ministry flowed—and continues to flow—from a posture of listening prayer.[40]

C. Listening to God Today

A hundred years have passed from the early days of the Alliance. Insights once learned need to be relearned and expanded in contemporary ways. Key areas that need contemporary development are: the phenomenology of listening to God, a well-formulated theology of listening to God, practical examples of listening prayer, true listening prayer being informed by the Word of God, "boundaries" in listening to God and how to make the transition from contemplation into action.

1. The Phenomenology of Listening to God

How does God speak to the child of God? Christians will sometimes say that God speaks to them by the Holy Spirit or by the Word of God. When asked to explain what they mean, they usually do not provide any convincing insights. They may say that God spoke to them through reading the Bible, hearing the preaching of the Word or having a verse of Scripture underlined to them by the Holy Spirit. They may add that understanding how God speaks majors on combining God's Word, the Holy Spirit, godly people and circumstances.[41] There is, however, something more to listening prayer than these aspects.

During listening prayer we can become suddenly aware of a flash of revelation, an insight in the form of a picture, an inner inaudible prompting, a thought that comes to mind, a word or phrase of Scripture that is continuously repeated, a prophetic word which begs to be uttered, a growing conviction or awareness of what needs to be done, an increasing consciousness of what God desires that just does not go away. We just know.

John Powell asks a series of rhetorical questions: Can God put a new idea directly and immediately into our *minds*? Can God give us a new perspective in which to view our lives with its successes and failures, agonies and ecstasies? Can God put new desires into our *hearts*, new strength into our *wills*? Can God touch and calm our turbulent *emotions*? Can God actually whisper words to the listening ears of our souls through the inner faculty of our *imaginations*? Can God stimulate certain *memories* stored within the human brain at the time these memories are needed?[42]

The following list describes over thirty ways God can communicate or speak with us, an enumeration of the multiple contexts in which God's message may be conveyed to us. We open up all the vents of our soul to hear God speaking to us. This list is only a beginning, for God can choose to speak to us any way God wants! As needed, God will confirm His speaking through a combination of various multiple means or an increasing unfolding. There are also boundaries or parameters, so we do not go astray. God can and does speak to us in multi-level methods as we open up all the vents of our soul to listen.[43]

> a. Bible—the purposeful, meditative spiritual reading and application of the Scriptures, and can include using the five senses of sight, hearing, smell, taste and touch.[44] *Lectio divina* or divine reading is sometimes described as "reading with the mind in the heart."[45] The written revelation of God's Word is combined together with the way the Holy Spirit quickens particular portions as a direct word in a present circumstance.[46]

> b. Preaching and Teaching—public presentation of the Word of God, applied by the Holy Spirit to the individual.

> c. Verbal Communication—an internal, inaudible message through a word or words spoken through the still, small voice of God, or perhaps, on occasion, the audible voice of God. This communication could be a specific Scripture, a statement, a question, a com-

mand. The *"still small voice"* in First Kings 19:12 (KJV) can also be translated "the sound of gentle stillness" or "a gentle whisper"; the Hebrew is literally "a voice, a small whisper."

d. Mental Pictures—inner picture-images or symbols, or messages as parables; a picture flashed across the inner screen of our mind.

e. Encounter—a phenomenal experience with God without words, but leaving an overwhelming message or strong impression.

f. Vision—a series of pictorial messages or visual images, literal or symbolic, while *awake*.[47] Visions may require some additional reflective and prayerful interpretation to discern their source and meaning.

g. Dream—a series of pictorial messages or visual images, literal or symbolic, while *asleep*. There are two formats of dreams—dreams arising from the subconscious mind that *God uses* to convey a message, and dreams that are directly heaven-sent *from God*. Dreams may require some additional reflective and prayerful interpretation.

h. Intellectual Reasoning—cognitive, mental processing and evaluating of data leading to clear conclusions, like connecting pieces of a puzzle.

i. Imagination—inner images or concepts creatively conceived or formed through guided imagery.

j. Intuition—knowing spontaneously the right thing to do or say.[48]

k. Conscience—knowing right from wrong. See Romans 2:15; 9:1.

l. Thoughts—ideas or principles, words or pictures that grow with increasing awareness, clarity, unfolding, intensity, conviction or volume in the mind.

m. Emotions—a gut-level feeling, desire, impulse, impression, arresting concern or insistent nudge.

n. Memory—the remembrance of an event, thought or Scripture previously learned. See John 2:22; 14:26.

o. Common Sense—the ordinary use of rational, good judgment through experience and logical thinking.

p. Observation—a quickening of insight when observing or reflecting on people, art or inanimate objects. For scriptural examples of listening to God by observing inanimate objects, see Jeremiah and the potter's wheel in Jeremiah 18:1-10; Amos and the plumb line in Amos 7:7-8; and Saul and Samuel's torn cloak in First Samuel 15:27-28.

q. Liturgy—a ritual ceremony or observance that emphasizes or drives home a certain reality or truth. The practice of the Lord's Supper is a profound example of this means of God's communication to us.

r. Nature—the silent shouting of God's creation, or inner messages that occur through ordinary created objects such as a flower or a tree. See Psalm 19:1-4.[49]

s. Circumstances—confirming situations and events that all seem to point in the same direction often combined with a profound sense of inner peace. See Colossians 3:15.

t. Signs and Wonders—external, more dramatic, supernatural and visible demonstrations of God's love and power to help, heal, care or deliver.

u. Pain—physical suffering serving as God's megaphone to gain our attention or teach some lesson.

v. Angels—messengers from God.

w. Theophany—a visible manifestation of God bringing a message. See Exodus 3:1-6.

x. Tongues and Interpretation—a spontaneous message from God in an unlearned language with interpretation in order to speak incisively to a situation, or bring immediate and profound comfort and peace to a person in distress.

y. Word of Wisdom—an appropriate, instantaneous insight for a particular occasion, to make a right decision, to discern good from evil, or to resolve, help or heal a particular situation or need.

z. Word of Knowledge—a fragment of knowledge or disclosure of truth implanted by God—not learned through the mind—about a particular person or situation for a specific purpose.

aa. Prophecy—a timely message or utterance through an individual from God to strengthen, encourage or comfort that person or that group of people at that particular time. See First Corinthians 14:3.

bb. Music—meditative or worshipful music that brings stillness, a sense of God's presence or a spirit of praise.

cc. Meditation—memorization, repetition and prayerful rumination of Scripture texts.

dd. Devotional Classics—a holy, super-slow reading of spiritual writings.

ee. Journaling—writing down times of communion or conversations with God.

ff. Soul Friends—spiritual mentors, godly friends or spouses who provide spiritual direction and counsel.[50]

gg. Collective Voice—the united voice and decision made by a group of believers.

What are the top three ways God frequently uses to speak to you? Which one is a current area of spiritual growth?

Not all of these ways of hearing God are necessarily God speaking. The rival voices we hear could be from our own self or from demonic sources. Nevertheless, God speaks in many ways if we will open up all the vents of our soul to listen. The secret is to sift through the many potential voices and hear the one thing God is saying in that present moment in whatever way God chooses to speak. However, Leanne Payne warns that we cannot turn listening prayer into a message-on-demand:

> As we simply allow time and space for God to speak, we learn both how easily and wonderfully the word comes and the differing ways it comes. . . . [I]t is with our *wills* . . . that we deliberately (*consciously*) open the eyes of our hearts and minds to receive the word God sends.[51]

Pardington described the phenomenology of listening to God through an analogy of the physical ear:

> In like manner, there is a spiritual sense of hearing; and upon this inner organ the holy accent of the voice of the Lord falls. Perhaps it is not so much a voice as a touch; a strange sweet sense of the contact of the Spirit of God with our spirit. Just as one can detect the presence of another in the room when he does not see him, so the believer whose inner spirit is sensitive and responsive knows the Master's voice when He speaks.[52]

Pardington also taught how to distinguish, through regular practice and through trial and error, the voice of the Lord from other voices, from oneself and from the voice of God's enemy. The voice of the enemy produces restlessness and prompts a great hurry to decide. The voice of the Lord produces rest and peace and gives time for one to think the matter over before coming to a decision. In ordinary affairs of life God may guide through the unconscious control of one's mental faculties. In more important matters, God will let His voice be heard. A quiet hour can begin with meditation on a passage of Scripture followed by the cultivation of the spirit of recollection. When God first speaks, we may not recognize God's voice; but if we patiently listen with a spirit ready instantly to obey, God will teach us the accent of God's voice and thus we will learn to walk by the Spirit.[53]

Listening to God, ultimately, is more than hearing a voice. It is an awareness that our thoughts and feelings are coming from God.[54] It is tuning into a multi-level mode of communication with God all day long as well as intensified as the present moment demands. It is an entering into a presence.[55] Ultimately, listening to God "is not a method, but a walk with a person."[56]

2. The Beginnings of a Theology of Listening to God

Listening prayer begins with the true self focusing on the true God as the object of one's contemplation. C.S. Lewis warned against egoistic subjectivism, when self talks to the self: "The prayer preceding all prayers is 'May it be the real I who speaks. May it be the real Thou that I speak to.' "[57] Undergirding listening prayer is a biblical theology of listening to God.[58]

> a. God has spoken through the Bible—2 Timothy 3:15-16; Hebrews 4:12.
>
> b. God has spoken through Jesus Christ—Matthew 17:5; John 1:14; Hebrews 1:1-2.
>
> c. God is still speaking—Acts 9:11-15; 1 Corinthians 14:26; Revelation 2:7a, 11a, 17a, 29; 3:6, 13, 22.
>
> d. God desires and invites people to listen—Genesis 28:16; Isaiah 55:3; Jeremiah 33:3; Matthew 11:15; James 1:5; Revelation 3:20.

e. God is displeased when people refuse to listen—Zechariah 7:11-13; Acts 28:26-27.

f. God makes the *logos* word a *rhema* word: the written word becomes a specific word for that situation—Habakkuk 2:1; Matthew 4:4; Romans 10:8, 17.

g. God's voice can be known—Exodus 33:11; 1 Samuel 3:8-10; 1 Kings 19:11-12; John 10:3-5, 8, 14, 27.

h. God's speaking is to lead to obedient action—John 2:5; Hebrews 3:7-8; James 1:22-25.

i. God communicates what to do and say when people listen—Isaiah 50:4-5; John 5:19; 8:28; 12:49-50.

Essentially, *God's voice* sounds like *God's character* which is most clearly revealed in *God's Word*. As we better understand God's Word and God's character, we get to know the divine presence speaking more clearly. God's voice will never contradict God's Word.

Many do not hear God speaking to them because they do not ask God questions that prompt a response, they do not expect God to give them any answers, they do not take time to listen, or they do not plan to obey what God tells them to do. Many do not connect the issues of their life or the world situations with God, yet this connecting is the normal interaction between God and the child of God. "To listen in prayer for the voice of the Lord is to find the mind of Christ; it is to gain transcendent wisdom, a wisdom that includes understanding, guidance, knowledge, exhortation, and consolation."[59] God is speaking; we can listen. We ask with Paul: *"What shall I do, Lord?"* (Acts 22:10, emphasis added).

3. Practical Examples of Listening Prayer

Theology moves into practice. God is trying to gain our attention. We need to put our ears on. Both Old and New Testaments provide biblical illustrations of listening prayer.

a. Samuel—"Speak, for your servant is listening" (1 Samuel 3:10).

b. Mary—"Mary . . . sat at the Lord's feet listening to what he said" (Luke 10:39).

c. Paul—"What shall I do, Lord?" (Acts 22:10).

Contemplative-active prayer is an Alliance heritage. These Alliance roots can be applied to today.

a. Intercessory Prayer—"God, how do You want me to pray? What can be done in this situation? Is there anything You would like me to do for this person to show them You are in control and that You care?"

b. Speaking to Others—"God, what tailor-made message needs to be spoken to someone for his or her encouragement?"

c. Sermon Preparation or Teaching—"God, what needs to be said now? How do You want me to say it?"

d. Leading Services—"God, what do You want to happen today among these Your people?"

e. The Ministry of Healing—"God, how do You want us to specifically pray for this person?"

f. The Academic Environment—"God, teach me how to be a whole person—balancing spiritual vitality, physical well-being, social development, psychological maturation and academic growth."

g. Public Conventions—"God, cause me to be drawn into silent waiting and expectation in order to increase my response to the preached Word."

h. Missionary Service—"God, where do You want me to go? Where do You want this person to serve?"

Listening prayer can further be applied in addressing contemporary questions. Begin by asking God questions! Come to God with a blank slate. Listen for answers! Always keep your ears open toward heaven. Plan to do whatever God tells you to do!

>a. Relationship with God—"God, what's the next step in my relationship with You?"

>b. Character Development—"God, what's the next step in the development of my character?"

>c. Family Life—"God, what's the next step in my family life?"

>d. Ministry—"God, what's the next step in my ministry?"

>e. Bible Reading—"God, what are You saying to me today? What are You saying to me through this passage?"

>f. Church Leadership—"God, what is Your vision for our church? What are You up to? How can we join it?"

>g. Scripting Difficult Relationships—"God, what do You want me to say, and how do You want me to say it? Give me the opening line. How do I start this conversation?"

>h. Other Questions—"God, what's the next step in my vocation? In my dating relationship? In my education?"[60]

4. Listening Prayer Informed by the Word of God

Listening prayer is also informed by the Word of God. Many commands throughout the Scriptures guide us. For example, the Gospel of Matthew records the high standards of discipleship in Jesus' Sermon on the Mount (5-7); the great commandments to love God and to love others (22:37-39); the call to meet the social needs of the hungry, the thirsty, the stranger, the needy, the sick, the imprisoned (25:34-40); the Great Commission to make disciples of all nations (28:18-20). Throughout the New Testament are "one another" commands intended for people-to-people ministry within the family of God. "The more learned we are in sound doctrine," Leanne Payne observes, "the greater our understanding of the Scriptures will be, and hence, of our listening to God through them."[61] If we are to do God's specific will, then we must first know God's general will.

In understanding the sacrament of the present moment, we learn to ask how we are to take all of these commands and directives of Scripture and apply them to ourselves and to our present moment now. What does God want us to do right now, this very moment? How can we carry out these timeless and authoritative directives specifically in our community and throughout our world? How does God want us to pray for this person? What phone call must be made right now? What conversation is to be initiated?

We have to acknowledge that we are far removed from the Bible in time, distance, language and culture. While the Bible is relevant for our lives today, how we *apply* biblical truth comes by listening to God in the present moment for that particular person or specific situation. "Listening to God is not about *newness* but about *nowness*," says Joyce Huggett. "It is receiving the applied Word in whatever form God chooses to make it known."[62] Sunder Krishnan has said, "Praying with a mind well-furnished with the plans and purposes of God revealed in the Scriptures is essential for an effective ministry of prayer and action, which unleashes the power of God into the human predicament."[63]

5. "Boundaries" in Listening to God

Opening all the vents of the soul to listen to God necessitates certain boundaries.

a. The "self" must be focused upon the Triune God of the Bible.

Listening prayer begins with the true self focusing on the true God as the object of one's contemplation. As already noted, C.S. Lewis warned against egoistic subjectivism, when self talks to the self: "The prayer preceding all prayers is 'May it be the real I who speaks. May it be the real Thou that I speak to.' "[64] We focus upon the Uncreated Creator, the Trinitarian God of both Old and New Testaments of the Bible, as revealed in the life, death and resurrection of Jesus Christ, and evidenced through the Holy Spirit.

b. The "mind" must be filled with the Word of God.

Whatever a mind is filled with will result in the product. The more we understand the Scriptures and sound doctrine, the greater will be our listening to God through them. If we are to do God's specific will applied in the *now*, then we must first know God's general will *already* revealed. Moreover, as the mind is anchored and *renewed* by the Word of God, we are more able to test and approve what God is saying (Romans 12:2).

c. The "channel" must be wholly sanctified in Jesus Christ.

Some people listen to and speak for God through a *rusty pipe*. What they hear God saying comes out cloudy and murky and usually requires some sorting out. There may be a genuine flow of God's living water coming through them, but it is mixed with themselves.

Other people are guilty of projecting their *well-wishes* upon others. They mean well, they have good intentions and they sound spiritual, but their words are not God speaking. They may be expressing their own agenda, because they have not died to their own agenda nor allowed God's true agenda to emerge.

Others who claim to speak for God have literally crossed the border into *witchcraft*. These people cannot be persuaded otherwise, for they believe God has spoken to them and to disagree with them, they feel, is to disagree with God. Supernatural guidance, however, is not the same as divine guidance.

Moreover, we cannot turn listening prayer into a message-on-demand. Nor can we dictate to God which method or combination of methods we want God to use to speak to us. Certainly, a recognition of these dangers provides cautionary boundary lines for the maturing believer. Jesus announced the key: "Blessed are the pure in heart, for they will see God" (Matthew 5:8). Like the hymn "Channels Only," the "channel" must be wholly sanctified in Jesus Christ in order for God's power to flow through to others.

d. The "test" of authenticity that we have heard from God must be confirmed through checks and balances.

God will often confirm and verify the divine speaking to us through various means. Sometimes, however, time alone proves its authenticity. We learn to walk by faith and take risks for God without all the answers or total understanding.

Learning to hear God speak is a *trial-and-error growth process*. It is grown sheep, and not lambs, that clearly hear God's voice. Yet even while we are growing spiritually, God will ensure that the divine message is understood and followed.

Sometimes people hear from God in a *Swiss cheese* format. What they perceive is from God, but the insight itself has some holes in it which need to be filled in with the insights of others. What they heard from God is not wrong, just incomplete, improper in that particular setting, or inappropriate at that particular time. This principle underlines the need for other gifted persons within the body of Christ to contribute their part to the whole.

God speaks to us on various levels of intensity for different situations. As needed, God will confirm His message through *multiple means, increasing unfolding,* and/or *through others,* e.g., new ministries are confirmed by church leadership. The more important God's Word to us, the greater measures God will use to make sure the divine speaking is clearly heard, understood and obeyed.

e. The "goal" of listening prayer must be for Christian living and effective ministry.

Guidance, direction, answers and insight are given by God for the sake of building up ourselves in our most holy faith, building up the body of Christ and extending the kingdom of God.

Our first priority and posture before God is to be like Mary, who was *absorbed in listening* at the feet of Jesus, rather than to be like Martha, who was *busy doing* and telling Jesus what her sister should be doing (Luke 10:38-42). Likewise, we do not consume ourselves telling Jesus what other Christians ought to be doing. Rather, our priority is in listening to God—taking in and reflecting upon what God would have us be and do.

In interpreting God's Word, we follow a threefold process of *observation, interpretation* and *application.* This same threefold process can apply to hearing God speak. At first God communicates to us some *insight*—what is the content of the message being revealed? Then we continue to listen to God for the practical *understanding* or increasing unfolding of that insight—what does that message mean? This is then followed by our obedient *outworking*—what does my response need to be now? Listening prayer is not complete until all three steps are fulfilled. Just as being busy doing for the Lord is not enough on the one hand, merely receiving and experiencing insight from the Lord is not enough on the other.

Listening prayer is a reflective kind of prayer with a purpose to hear from the Lord for specific action. We ask with Paul: "What shall I do, Lord?" (Acts 22:10).

6. Making the Transition from Contemplation into Action

Making the transition from contemplation into action is difficult for some.[65] The goal for those in ministry is to approach all that we do from the center of our union with God.[66] From that center we set specific listening and action as our goal. David Hassel asks, "Could it even be that, deep within, we each feel God quietly encouraging us to stretch our lives out to others?" [67] The feeling grows from within that we want and need to do something for God and for people. It is God calling and leading us to an outward journey of faith.

Passing through an apprentice stage of development in listening prayer equips us to effectively listen when a specific occasion arises. We need only to look heavenward, pause for silence, breathe a prayer to God and listen quietly for direction. How do we respond to the person at the door or on the phone? What do we underscore to this couple sitting in front of us for marriage counseling?[68] How can we pray for this person who is sick?[69] To what sphere of social ministry is God calling this local congregation? How can a small group pray on target for various needs that emerge? What is God calling our church to do within our community and our world? These answers are found through listening to God through prayer. The more profound the need, the longer the time needed for careful listening.

> To walk in the Spirit, listening, is to live in the present moment, looking to Christ, practicing his presence, moving in tandem with God. It is to live from the locus of the true self as the old one is being crucified. This is the center where we are in union with Christ, that completed self that hears and obeys God.[70]

From that center of deep heart-awareness of God and His people, the indwelling Trinity's presence permeates and "rises slowly through the contemplative's whole being so that his or her arms can go out in self-forgetting welcome to God and his world."[71]

Conclusion

Listening prayer is essential for effective ministry. A mind attuned to the Word of God, an affection leaning on the heart of God and a will listening to the Spirit of God lead the believer in Jesus Christ to hear from God. Hearing from God leads the ordinary believer to minister the grace of God into needy lives and a needy world. Listening to God in order to do ministry is the normative pattern of the Christian life and was the historic practice in early Alliance spirituality.

Endnotes

[1] Thomas Keating, "Centering Prayer," *The New Dictionary of Catholic Spirituality*, ed. Michael Downey (Collegeville, MI: The Liturgical Press, 1993), 138-139.

[2] A.B. Simpson, *The Holy Spirit or Power from on High: Part I. The Old Testament*, hereafter cited *HS:OT* (New York: The Christian Alliance Publishing Co., 1924), 160.

[3] A.B. Simpson, *The Holy Spirit or Power from on High: Part II. The New Testament* (Harrisburg, PA: Christian Publications, Inc., 1896), 73.

[4] Comparative, contemporary analysis on listening prayer is drawn primarily from Joyce Huggett, *Listening to God*, hereafter cited *LTG* (London: Hodder and Stoughton, 1986), 53-74.

[5] Also see Leonard Doohan, "6 Aids to Blocks to a Leisured Approach to Prayer," in *Leisure: A Spiritual Need* (Notre Dame: Ave Maria Press, 1990), 77-85.

[6] G.P. Pardington, *The Still Small Voice: Quiet Hour Talks*, hereafter cited *SSV*, (New York: Christian Alliance Publishing Co., 1902), 113.

[7] Charles de Foucauld quoted in *LTG*, 117.

[8] *SSV*, 123-124.

[9] A.B. Simpson, "Breathing Out and Breathing In," in *Hymns of the Christian Life*, rev. ed., hereafter cited, *HCL*. (Harrisburg, PA: Christian Publications, Inc., 1978), 251.

[10] See Leanne Payne, *Listening Prayer: Learning to Hear God's Voice and Keep a Prayer Journal*, hereafter cited *LP*. (Grand Rapids, MI: Baker Books, 1994), 130-132, 135-138. Payne affirms this by calling God "the Objective Real."

[11] *HS:OT*, 161.

[12] Richard W. Bailey, "The Alliance's Theologian," *The Alliance Witness* (8 October 1986): 24.

[13] See *SSV*, 122-123.

[14] *HCL*, 217, 235, 239.

[15] A.B. Simpson, *Higher and Deeper* (South Nyack, NY: The Christian Alliance Publishing Co., n.d.), 40.

[16] A.B. Simpson, "The Secret of Prayer," *Living Truths* 4 (March 1904): 121; quoted in Dwayne Ratzlaff, "An Old Mediaeval Message: A Turning Point in the Life of A. B. Simpson," hereafter cited *OMM*, in *The Birth of a Vision*, eds., David F. Hartzfeld and Charles Nienkirchen. (Beaverlodge, Alberta: Buena Book Services, 1986), 176.

[17] For example, see A.B. Simpson, *The Four-Fold Gospel* (Harrisburg, PA: Christian Publications, Inc., n.d.), 65-66.

[18] *HS:OT*, 162.

[19] I expand this dimension of listening prayer within the Alliance in the next major section.

20   William H. Shannon, "Contemplation, Contemplative Prayer," *The New Dictionary of Catholic Spirituality*, ed., Michael Downey (Collegeville, MN: Liturgical Press, 1993), 209.

21   *LTG*, 207.

22   *OMM*, 186-187.

23   A.B. Simpson, "Editorial," *Living Truths* (July 1906): 385; quoted in *OMM*, 187.

24   *SSV*, 17.

25   A.B. Simpson, "Editorial," *The Christian Alliance and Foreign Missionary Weekly* 12 (February 16, 1894): 1; and A.B. Simpson, *Practical Christianity* (Brooklyn, NY: The Christian Alliance Publishing Co., 1901), 61-62.

26   A.E. Thompson, "17. A Pauline Mystic," in *A.B. Simpson: His Life and Work* Revised Edition (Harrisburg, PA: Christian Publications, Inc., 1960), 171-183.

27   *SSV*, 12-13.

28   *OMM*, 176.

29   *SSV*, 107.

30   *SSV*, 167-168.

31   *SSV*, 170.

32   *OMM*, 170.

33   See Robert L. Niklaus, John S. Sawin and Samuel J. Stoesz, *All For Jesus: God at Work in The Christian and Missionary Alliance Over One Hundred Years* (Camp Hill, PA: Christian Publications, Inc., 1986), 124, 271.

34   Kenneth Mackenzie, Jr., *Divine Life for the Body* (NY: The Christian Alliance Publishing Co., 1926), 145-147.

35   Sarah Lindenberger, *Streams from the Valley of Berachah* (NY: The Christian Alliance Publishing Co., n.d.), 124.

36   Sarah Lindenberger, "The Work of Berachah Home," *The Christian Alliance and Missionary Weekly* 4 (21-28 March 1890): 207.

37   *The Nyack Schools of The Christian and Missionary Alliance (1914-1915) Catalogue Nyack-on-Hudson* (n.p., n.d.), 7; and *Manual of The New York Missionary Training Institute, Nyack Heights, Nyack, New York* (1911) (n.p., n.d.), 8, 26.

38   George Pardington, *Twenty-Five Wonderful Years 1889-1914* (NY: The Christian Alliance Publishing Co., 1914), 78-80.

39   *SSV*, 75-76.

40   Our local ministerial *almost* entered into a frightful expenditure of tens of thousands of dollars without so much as an ounce of prayer regarding the endeavor. Fortunately, we were later clearheaded enough to humble ourselves, admit our folly, rescind former motions and learn from our experience. Now we are committed to an unfolding vision that is emerging through listening prayer.

41   See Charles Stanley, *How to Listen to God* (Nashville, TN: Thomas Nelson Publishers, 1985), 7-18.

42   John Powell, *He Touched Me* (Chicago: Argus Publications, 1974), 70. Emphasis his.

[43] Though these concepts are not unique, this listing is original with me. There are probably an unlimited number of ways God speaks to us. Any attempt to categorize and describe the phenomenon of listening to God tends to fall short, because there always remains a mystical element.

[44] The use of the five senses was particularly incorporated by Ignatius of Loyola.

[45] *LTG*, 159.

[46] *LP*, 178.

[47] Leanne Payne defines a vision as "a heightened consciousness of another realm. . . . A realm that is ordinarily unseen is extraordinarily present to the senses." *LP*, 185. The word "vision" is understood in a variety of ways. One way to categorize visions is to differentiate between literal visual appearances or apparitions of God or angelic beings, pictures or images that appear within the imagination, and abstract concepts that develop within the intellect.

[48] Simpson wrote, "The thoughts come as our own . . . a sort of intuition that it is the right thing to do. . . . It is not so much the Spirit speaking to us as the Spirit speaking with us as part of our very consciousness, so that it is not two minds, but one." A.B. Simpson, *Walking in the Spirit* (Harrisburg, PA: Christian Publications, Inc., n.d.), 39; quoted in *OMM*, 175.

[49] God spoke to our family in July 1995 through the demonstration of the power of God. A tall, thick tree blew down in our backyard during a violent windstorm. A tree that had stood for years, around 30" in diameter, was snapped off in a few seconds. Some would have viewed this as a natural phenomenon. Others would have felt helpless over the destructiveness of nature. My wife and I both felt that God used it to speak of the overwhelming power of God in a specific situation we were facing at the time.

[50] God often speaks to me through my wife. I have learned to pay close attention to what she is saying, for God may be using her words to get through to me.

[51] *LP*, 159.

[52] *SSV*, 56-57.

[53] See *SSV*, 56-64, 93-94, 97-107.

[54] Frank Wallace, "6. Surprise Discoveries Start with Listening," *Encounter Not Performance* (Australia: E. J. Dwyer, 1991), 43.

[55] *LTG*, 33, 185-186.

[56] *LP*, 121.

[57] C.S. Lewis, *Letters to Malcolm: Chiefly on Prayer* (New York: Harcourt, Brace & World, Inc., 1964), 82, hereafter cited *LM*. See also *LP*, 209-218.

[58] Again, this listing is original with me. The Scripture references are not intended to be proof texts, but representative, guiding and supportive verses.

[59] *LP*, 125.

[60] Some of these contemporary questions are from Bill Hybels, *Honest to God? Becoming an Authentic Christian* (Grand Rapids, MI: Zondervan Publishing House, 1990), 24-26.

[61] *LP*, 253. See also page 27.

[62] *LTG*, 91.

[63] Sunder Krishnan, "First Principles Forum," Ravi Zacharias International Ministries, February 1997.

[64] *LP*, 82.

[65] This is not a primary concern for Ignatian spirituality which has always emphasized contemplation in action beginning with its founder. The Society of Jesus emphasizes that the primary means to deeper union with God is achieved through purity of heart and accompanied through service to others. See Robert J. Wicks, ed., *Handbook of Spirituality for Ministers* (New York: Paulist Press, 1995), 223-224, 278.

[66] See Joyce Rupp, "17. Rediscovering God in the Midst of our Work," in *Handbook of Spirituality for Ministers*, Robert J. Wicks, ed. (New York: Paulist Press, 1995), 259-273.

[67] David Hassel, "5. Prayer of Apostolic Contemplation-In-Action: Welcoming Christ and His World," in *Radical Prayer: Creating a Welcome for God, Ourselves, Other People and the World* (New York: Paulist Press, 1984), 71, hereafter cited *RP*. Hassel correlates and differentiates the secular, religious and apostolic contemplative, the latter reflecting contemplation-in-action. See *RP*, 62-80.

[68] Henry Nouwen writes that it is "possible to experience the relationship between pastor and counselee as a way of entering together into the loving silence of God and waiting there for the healing Word." See Henri M. Nouwen, "Silence, the Portable Cell," *Sojourners* (July 1980): 22.

[69] The Christian and Missionary Alliance is not a Pentecostal denomination, but it believes in divine healing. Its Statement of Faith reads: "8. Provision is made in the redemptive work of the Lord Jesus Christ for the healing of the mortal body. Prayer for the sick and anointing with oil as taught in the Scripture are privileges for the Church in this present age." This emphasis is based on Scriptures such as Matthew 8:16-17 and James 5:14-16. I made a hospital visit to a parishioner in his late seventies who had experienced a heart attack. While driving to the hospital, I asked God how to pray for him. I sensed very clearly that this was not his time to die. I prayed for a quick recovery and added years to his life. He was very soon out of the hospital, unbelievably back in church the following Sunday and claims today with tears in his eyes that his recovery was a miracle.

[70] *LP*, 148.

[71] *RP*, 80.

Designer Genes[1]: Some Ethical Issues in the Genetic Manipulation of Man

Matthew A. Cook

Genetic engineering excites emotions among religious leaders and ethicists. Many of the articles and books that are being produced follow one of two patterns. Either they present it under the overcast sky of "greed and gloom" or they present it amidst the glowing aura of "gee whiz."[2]

Regardless of one's emotional response, genetic engineering may be *the* crucial issue for the Church to address in the twenty-first century.[3] This is a reasonable prediction, for there is a growing list of maladies and calamities that have been found to be genetically related, including many of the most dreaded diseases of our time, such as Huntington's, sickle-cell anemia, muscular dystrophy, diabetes, heart disease and its antecedents, arthritis, cystic fibrosis and various forms of cancer. In addition, there are a host of lesser-known but serious—even deadly—ailments that have a genetic component.

Should not the Church take a stand for the elimination of these diseases? By what means and for what purpose are these diseases to be eliminated? These are the crucial questions.

To begin this discussion I must define some terms. Then I will discuss three of the techniques of genetic manipulation: gene therapy, germ-line manipulation and eugenics.

Defining Terms

A *gene* is defined as a particular nucleotide sequence. This sequence dictates the particular protein produced that (usually) is the significant element in altering the biological characteristics of an organism. It works like this: DNA is made up of building blocks (nucleotides); these nucleotides bond with specific amino acids; the order of the nucleotides (a gene) determines the order of the amino acids (the protein). Genetic manipulation is all about changing the order of the nucleotides so that a different effect is obtained in the body.[4]

Positive genetic manipulation is the use of genetic techniques to accomplish some improvement in the individual or the human race as a whole. It has been called progressive eugenics because the scientist (or society) is viewed as making progress through the use of genetic manipulation.[5]

Negative genetic manipulation does not indicate a negative assessment of genetics at all. Rather, it is the use of genetic techniques to repair or prevent some misfortune, some defect or some disease from occurring. In this regard it has been called preventive eugenics.[6]

Unfortunately, there is no clear dividing line between positive and negative categories, even though much discussion is carried on using these terms. Consider what the distinction is. Either the dividing line between these two goals is the mean (average) of some people (hence, there is one objective standard by which all people are measured) or it is different for every person. If the mean is the dividing line then one faces the thorny problem of knowing what constituents one should use for averaging. Perhaps one should take the average of all Mensa members, or the average of everyone who has achieved a Ph.D., or the average of everyone who makes more than $100,000 per year, etc. This "averaging" is implicit in some of the literature. Consider the following definition of a mutation: "an alteration of nucleotide sequence."[7] But everyone's nucleotide sequence is different!

> In examining the DNA of different individuals, researchers will be confronted by the full range of genetic variations among persons. What constitutes a genetic defect, and what constitutes genetic variation? ... What is a defect in one society is a desirable characteristic in another.[8]

Even if we knew what was most common we would not know (except through society's judgment) which way is up and which way is down. In effect there is no *scientific* way of drawing a clear line between positive and negative genetic manipulation. This inability should induce caution and continued reflection on the question, "Toward what end is one using genetic manipulation?"

If no one can define a universal standard of the correct or best nucleotide sequence (read "body")—and I doubt they can—then one is left with an individualistic line. This line is now legitimate *only* for persons to apply to themselves and is not legitimate for any person to apply to any other person. Without an objective standard, no person can say that another person does not measure up because they have not answered the more basic question: measure up to *what*? No hierarchy can impose legitimate rules for, say, nonvoluntary sterilization or the like. I am advocating a clear plurality of the gene pool, an unashamed diversity in the human race that can be expected from our creative God.

It is possible, of course, that the person in favor of positive genetic manipulation could urge us to raise the overall average of our population. But which way is up? Some may value winning the Olympics; others may value a small physique. Some may value individuals with great academic potential; others may value individuals who remain in the community to improve it. Some may like a slim waist; others may value enough girth to endure a more difficult life. Each society may have different criteria of perfection.

Genetic engineering, therefore, should be treated like any other medical advance: to be accepted or rejected by the patient in question. In genetic engineering, I am *pro-choice*, but not like the pro-choice camp of abortion. In the abortion issue, pro-choice means one person's choice produces the death of another. I advocate each individual having the privilege to chose or reject genetic therapy based on his or her culture or circumstances. Already from this discussion I have purposefully prejudiced the case of whether or not to accept some of the options yet to be presented.

Three Techniques of Genetic Manipulation

1. Human Gene Therapy

Human gene therapy is intended to cure a genetic disease in a specific body tissue.[9] This runs the gamut of applications, from treating an infant's hereditary disorder with fetal tissue to changing a cancer cell so that it produces its own anti-tumor.

In fact, the two examples just cited have been performed recently. The infant in question was born in 1990 to a couple who had lost two children to Hurler Syndrome, a genetic abnormality that deprives the body of a single critical enzyme, producing skeletal problems and severe mental retardation.[10] The newborn was also deficient in the necessary enzyme, indicating Hurler Syndrome. Dr. Esmail Zanjani obtained tissue recovered from an aborted fetus and injected it into the infant. A magazine article on the procedure later reported that "Five to 10 percent of the child's blood-making cells are descendants of the transplanted cells."[11] While the final results are not in, there is hope that this child may not develop the symptoms associated with Hurler Syndrome.

The second example occurred in 1991. Dr. Steven Rosenberg injected into a melanoma cancer patient a cell containing the gene that promotes an anti-tumor hormone called tumor necrosis factor (TNF). Because the cell had earlier been extracted from the very same patient, it was fully compatible with the surrounding cells—except that it contained the altered gene. The results are not yet known.[12]

The argument for this technique of genetic manipulation is strong: We heal individuals by using drugs, machines and operations; why not also use genetic means? It could be seen as an extension of drugs, since in many cases the body is in need of a particular hormone, enzyme or other chemical compound that physicians are unable to supply from the outside. Through gene therapy, they are able to supply it "from the inside," i.e., they are able to manipulate a cell so that it produces the needed chemical while resident in the patient's body. This technique can be seen as an extension of the healing art of the physician.

The arguments against human gene therapy are common to both this technique and one which will be discussed later:

(1) Is this "playing God"? No, this is no more "playing God" than injecting an antibiotic for pneumonia is "playing God."

(2) Is there a danger that one of these artificially created molecules will escape and create an epidemic of catastrophic proportions? (In the literature this is referred to as the "Andromeda Strain" scenario.) That is a possibility, though it is highly unlikely. Researchers are confident that current containment methods are sufficient to make the risk worthwhile.

(3) Does this technology sometimes require embryo research or tissue from embryos? Certainly, sometimes embryo tissue is used.[13] And this does present a significant ethical problem for the technique.

The couple whose infant was treated with fetal tissue viewed the embryo from whom the tissue was taken as already dead, whether or not the medical procedure was performed. Their doctor even said, "I know it's crude to say it—one life to save five, if successful." They do not consider the future use of that tissue as a driving factor toward increasing the number of abortions. The important element from this is that another child (or more than one) will live.

I wonder if perhaps they are correct. Could tissue use possibly influence potential abortion clients toward abortion? Not likely. Would not this use of the tissue be salvaging at least some good from an otherwise horrible situation? Yes. But the use of fetal tissue may influence legislators or lobbyists in any future debates over the legalization of abortion.

Consider a future scenario where aborted fetal tissue is regularly used for gene therapy and legislation is proposed to outlaw abortion. Not only would "pro-choice" advocates be as vocal as ever, but medical advocates would be just as vocal—and with a stronger argument than ever before: that abortions can *save* lives! For this reason, I do not advocate using embryonic or fetal tissue for genetic therapy.

On the other hand, shall we just stand by and let a Hurler Syndrome baby die? Not at all; there are other options. Researchers are now able to remove tissue from a patient, genetically alter it, grow more cells in the lab, and then reinject the tissue into the patient's body.[14] A group of scientists in Ohio has even assembled an artificial human chromosome for more efficient delivery of therapeutic genes to a patient's cells.[15] There are applications of gene therapy where fetal tissue is not involved at all.[16]

I have only mentioned negative or preventive gene therapy to this point. Positive or progressive gene therapy can take the form of altering the genes of an individual to improve that person beyond the norm. This application has not received much effort because the effect would exist only for that person; there would be no lasting improvement in the human gene pool (that is part of a technique we will look at later).

Discussions of positive gene therapy have typically been in the context of inappropriate exploitation or manipulation. Examples could include an athlete trying to become a world-class sprinter by taking steroids, or a country trying to win an Olympic basketball championship by "growing" their own team through regular injections of height hormones. Perhaps another application would be to "trick" some genes into thinking that the body is younger than it is so that the cells of a seventy-year-old begin repairing and reproducing themselves at the rate of a twenty-year-old. These examples play with nature for personal advantage. They represent a contemporary form of the self-aggrandizement the Bible so frequently characterizes as sin (e.g., in 1 Chronicles 21 when David commanded a census to be taken and Acts 8:9-25 which relates the incident of Simon the magician).

2. Human Germ-line Research

Lewis P. Bird argues, "If it is biologically and morally permissible to cure diabetes in a patient, why is it somehow inherently immoral to cure such a disease in one's offspring?"[17] Germ-line research would result in changing the genetic code of an individual so that his natural descendants would also feel the effects of that change. This involves rearranging the elements of the DNA so that they produce the appropriate proteins for the desired effect. This was not possible until a big breakthrough came in the 1970s at CalTech, where, according to Dennis Chamberland, "One machine automatically identified the sequence of cellular amino acids, spelling out the DNA code of the particular gene. Another machine assembled artificial genes piece by piece."[18]

Germ-line research is available for either negative or positive genetic manipulation. Negatively, it could be used as Lewis Bird advocates, to engineer out "defects" from the human genetic pool. Positively, it could be used to engineer "advances" in humanity—desirable traits such as intelligence, height and hair color. It could even develop potentially necessary traits, such as resistance to UV radiation.

The argument for germ-line research follows that of Lewis Bird: If we can reduce the genetic load of imperfections on our descendants then we have an obligation to do that very thing. The possibilities are awe-inspiring. The potential before us has to do with improving ourselves—and not just ourselves, but all of our descendants. Each of us wants to make a contribution for the good of society and our progeny. Here is a possibility to do that very thing: to improve the lot of those who come after us, to raise their life above the suffering of our own, to eliminate the pain of genetic disease, to raise our race to a new level of existence. That seems to be a worthy endeavor.

The main argument against germ-line research is that most of the underlying genetic factors for genetic diseases are polygenetic in origin.[19] Beyond that, this technique does not take into account the interaction between nature and nurture influences.[20] Stephen Stich, as well as many other researchers, points out that only to a very limited extent do we "understand how nature and nurture conspire to produce complex mental and behavioral traits."[21] That same author states the unreasonableness of trying to engineer in or out personality traits.

> "Feeblemindedness" is like dirt. It is not one thing,
> but many unrelated things; it is no more plausible to
> suppose we could discover laws or theories about fee-

blemindedness than it is to think we might discover laws and theories about dirt.[22]

Stich contends that many characteristics fall into this category: success, intelligence, ability, feeblemindedness, criminality.[23] But this complexity is not limited to lifestyle characteristics; as I indicated above, even the so-called genetic diseases are often the result of multi-genetic effects.

A second argument against this technique is that the extent to which we are pursuing improvement will skew our understanding of children. Allen Verhey has said this very well:

> The technologies are introduced to increase our options, to get us what we want, a healthy [or improved] child. But if parenting is to make parents happy, then genetic engineering will go foul because we will abort whatever or whomever does not meet our specifications—and still be unhappy. And if parenting is to make children happy, then genetic engineering will still go foul because the awesome responsibility to minimize their suffering and to maximize their happiness will have a self-stimulating impetus until we have reduced our options to a perfect child or a dead child. . . . But to assume a responsibility to produce "perfect" children or to assure their "happiness" will drive joy out of parenting and compassion out of children.[24]

"Such utilitarian approaches may be fine for cows and corn," comments John Kilner, "but human beings, made in the image of God, have a God-given dignity that prevents us from regarding other people merely as means to fulfill our desires."[25]

A third argument against this technique is that progress rarely finds itself satisfied. This is a form of the practical "slippery slope" argument.[26] First, although technologies are initially introduced to "increase our options," they can quickly become socially enforced. Consider the automobile. At first it was a mere convenience, but now it is inconceivable to maneuver through many of our lives without one. Second, although technologies are introduced to make things we want, they seldom satisfy our wants. Although the car is faster than the horse, we want even faster cars. Even though genetic manipulation may eliminate some diseases, we might want to use it to move man toward "perfection." Third, although technology has brought good and significant benefits, it can be used, in Allen Verhey's words, for "greed and pride and envy."[27]

A fourth argument against this technique is that it involves experimentation on human fetuses and experimental techniques of *in vitro* fertilization. While *in vitro* fertilization is not bad in itself it is unlikely that germ-line research can be introduced through *in vitro* fertilization without a significant number of trials and failures, resulting in aborted fetuses. Listen to the process as described by Jonathan King:

> In the test tube one can introduce DNA or cells altered in the laboratory into this early embryo and then implant the embryo back into the womb. From this is the possibility . . . [of changing] the germ-line cells. Thus the changes would be passed to subsequent generations.[28]

Unfortunately, the process involves many trials using embryos that were only partially successful and must be destroyed or using parts of embryos that are destroyed in the process. Similar issues affect cloning:

> In the process used to clone sheep [a.k.a. Dolly], there were 227 failed attempts—including the deaths of several defective clones. In the monkey-cloning process, a living embryo was intentionally destroyed by taking the genetic material from the embryo's eight cells and inserting it into eight egg cells whose partial genetic material had been removed. Human embryos and human infants would likewise be lost as the technique is adapted to our own race.[29]

This *in vitro* abortion is unacceptable. My understanding of the reproductive process is that life begins at conception. That means that the image of God and the soul are already resident. God makes clear His demand to protect those who are created in His image (Genesis 9:6).

There are too many detrimental possibilities with this technique to warrant an enthusiastic response. Neither negative germ-line research nor positive germ-line research offer much promise. Certainly the positive goal must be eschewed for the social implications and the difficulty of defining how the genetic change can be complemented by the environmental change. Even if the negative goal may at some future time be shown to offer hope of eliminating some disease through minimal manipulation it still presents too many deleterious side effects and requires research methods which are too abhorrent to warrant the benefit.[30] I agree with 1980 Nobel laureate Jean Dausset: "Thus as things stand at present, germ-line therapy must be strictly banned."[31]

3. Eugenics

Eugenics is described as the selection and recombination of genes already existing in the human gene pool. Negative eugenics aims at removing the deleterious genes; positive or progressive eugenics tries to spread superior genes.[32] The negative option can be accomplished through a number of means: sterilization of the retarded (either forced or voluntary); amniocentesis followed by abortion of "defective" fetuses; and genetic screening programs, resulting in reproductive abstinence of those found with genetic "defects."

Positive eugenics is accomplished through the widespread use of those persons' genes who happen to have received more than their share of "valuable" genes. It is in this context that H.J. Muller is often mentioned. Muller, a Nobel laureate, proposed a sperm bank for Nobel laureates. From that bank any female desiring to improve the genetic pool of the human race could be artificially inseminated.[33]

The main argument for eugenics is to spread the influence of advanced genes or eliminate the spread of "defective" genes through a social selection that will pick up where natural selection has been circumvented. As Muller stated his "ethics of genetic duty":

> Although it is a human right for people to have their infirmities cared for by every means that society can muster, they do not have the right knowingly to pass on to posterity such a load of infirmities of genetic or partly genetic origin as to cause an increase in the burden already being carried by the population.[34]

Because the negative and positive forms of this technique form somewhat different problems, I will deal with them separately.

The first argument against positive eugenics is that it promotes a distorted purpose for children. Although a firm definition cannot be placed on the purpose for children I contend that their purpose is not that of pawns for the improvement of the race. They are not objects, even for the spread of "good" genes. They are not to be "perfect."

When speaking of high-tech methods of conception that are frequently necessary in eugenics, Christian ethicist Gilbert Meilaender says, "In general, and even entirely apart from the use of donated sperm or eggs, it becomes increasingly difficulty to think of the child as a gift and not a product."[35] The "product" model is directly antithetical to Psalm 127:3-5.

The second argument against positive eugenics is the intermixture between the influences of nature and nurture to produce desirable effects. There can be no guarantee that our work in eugenics will produce anything like the desired result.

The arguments against negative eugenics are not against the goal but against some of the methods that are used to accomplish the task. I agree that genetic counseling should be available to every individual. But social pressure or forced sterilization is inappropriate because that would impose someone else's criteria of what is "normal" and what is "deficient" upon free individuals. Another inappropriate method of implementation of this technique is amniocentesis with abortion of "defective" fetuses. It is in this context that Verhey says we end up with either a "perfect child or a dead child."[36]

Conclusion

This initial investigation into genetic engineering reveals some significant problems with many areas of application. There are four great difficulties with genetic engineering:

1. Sometimes one person (or group) tries to define the line between negative and positive genetic manipulation, in effect determining who is "deficient" and who is "sufficient." These kinds of labels are inappropriate for both our pluralistic society and a Christian conception of the image of God resident in an individual (Genesis 1:26, 27).

2. Any attempt to engineer "out" or "in" a certain characteristic is often complicated by the difficult interaction between genetics and the environment.

3. Many of the techniques necessary to conduct genetic research and treatment are unethical (by my standards). The end does not justify the means because those who bear the harm (usually aborted fetuses) have no hope of benefit from the techniques.

4. The goals toward which genetic engineering is striving are sometimes inappropriate.

Genetic manipulation will become more common with the advance of science. The Human Genome Project[37] (funded by the federal government) is currently mapping the 3 billion units of DNA that constitute the genetic programming of human cells.[38] Their purpose is to provide a comprehensive mapping of genes. There are competitive commercial ventures paralleling the Genome Project. Their purpose is to prepare and market genetic therapy to change one's genetic code.[39] Sometimes those techniques will be useful, but the Christian community must come to some significant and difficult conclusions about the value of individuals based solely on the presence of the image of God (regardless of their intellectual, athletic or social abilities), the rights of individuals to make choices for themselves and the complex implications of genetic manipulation.

Genetic Manipulation: A Summary of Techniques Discussed

(Those portions this author finds as unacceptable are italicized.)

	Negative—reduce harm and "defects"	Positive—increase "desirables"
Gene Therapy	Fix **many** plaguing genetic diseases for the affected person	*Growth hormones* *Steroids*
Germ-line	*"Engineer out" dominant recessive "defects."* Acceptable if techniques advance to alter monogenetic diseases without purposeful embryonic deaths.	*"Engineer in" desirable traits:* • *Intelligence* • *Hair color* • *UV radiation resistance*

	Negative—reduce harm and "defects"	Positive—increase "desirables"
Eugenics	Inhibit those with genetic deficiencies from reproducing: • Genetic counseling • *Forced* or voluntary sterilization	*Muller's sperm bank to spread the influence of "superior genes"* *Cloning*

Endnotes

1   Taken from Allen Verhey, "The Morality of Genetic Engineering," *Christian Scholar's Review* 14 (1985): 125, hereafter cited *MG*.

2   Stephen P. Stick, "The Rewards and Risks of Studying Genes," *The Hastings Center Report* 16 No.2 (April 1986): 39, hereafter cited *RRSG*.

3   This is a paraphrase of a comment made by John S. Feinberg in personal conversation with the author.

4   Lee Ehrman and Joe Grossfield, et al., "The Supreme Court and Patenting Life," *The Hastings Center Report* 10 (October 1980): 10, hereafter cited *SCPL*.

5   Paul Ramsey, "Moral and Religious Implications of Genetic Control," in *On Moral Medicine: Theological Perspectives in Medical Ethics*, ed. Stephen E. Lammers and Allen Verey (Grand Rapids, MI: Eerdmans, 1987), 370, hereafter cited *MRIGC*.

6   Ibid., 370.

7   Ehrman and Grossfield, *SCPL*, 10.

8   Jonathan King, "Prospects and Hazards of New Genetic Technologies," *Christianity and Crisis: A Christian Journal of Opinion* 39 (October 15, 1979): 251, hereafter cited *PHNGT*.

9   Ronald S. Cole-Turner, "Is Genetic Engineering Co-creation?" *Theology Today* 44 (October 1987): 340.

10   *The Chicago Tribune*, Associated Press Story, 10 October 1991. Sec. 1. Page 3.

11   Ibid.

12   Anastasia Toufexis, *TIME*, 21 October 1991.

13   See above, the example of the child with Hurler Syndrome. The article was written in the context of the parents being called to testify at congressional hearings in April, 1991 on the subject of fetal tissue research.

14   Roberta Hubbord and John Ettorre, "Hopeful Expression: In Gene Therapy, Researchers Probe the Potential of a Breakthrough Medical Treatment. Their Aim Is

Nothing Less Than the Conquest of Genetically Based Diseases," *CWRU* [a publication of Case Western Reserve University] (February 1995): 10.

15   Kristin Ohlson, "Divide and Conquer," *CWRU* (May 1998): 14.

16   See above, where the cancer patient was injected with his own genetically altered cells.

17   Lewis Bird, "Universal Principles of Biomedical Ethics and Their Application to Gene-splicing," *Perspectives on Science and Christian Faith: Journal of the American Scientific Affiliation* 41 (June 1989): 85.

18   Dennis Chamberland, "Genetic Engineering: Promise and Threat," *Christianity Today* 30:2 (February 7, 1986): 24.

19   Marc Lappe, "The Predictive Power of the New Genetics," *The Hastings Center Report* 14 (October 1984): 19.

20   Cloning cultural heroes forces the same issue. "They, like us, were shaped by genetics and environment alike, with the spiritual capacity to evaluate, disregard, and at times to overcome either or both." John Kilner, "Stop Cloning Around," *Christianity Today*, 41 (28 April 1997), 11, hereafter cited *SCA*.

21   Stick, *RRSG*, 40.

22   Ibid., 41.

23   Ibid.

24   Verhey, *MG*, 136-7.

25   Kilner, *SCA*, 10.

26   This argument and analogy is largely taken from Verhey, 134.

27   Ibid., 134.

28   King, *PHNGT*, 251.

29   Kilner, *SCA*, 10.

30   Note also the discussion by Allen Verhey on compensatory justice. With germ-line research those who suffer the greatest risk have no hope of reaping any of the benefit for they are dead. Verhey, 128-132.

31   Jean Dausset, "Scientific Knowledge and Human Dignity," *Unesco Courier*, 47 (September 1994), 10.

32   Charles E. Curran, "Moral Theology and Genetics," in *On Moral Medicine: Theological Perspectives in Medical Ethics*, ed. Stephen E. Lammers and Allen Verhey (Grand Rapids, MI: Eerdmans, 1987), 373.

33   Ramsey, *MRIGC*, 368.

34   H. J. Muller, *Man's Future Birthright*. (University of New Hampshire, Feb. 1958), 18. As quoted in Ramsey, 371.

35   Gilbert Meilaender, "Biotech Babies," *Christianity Today*, 42 (7 December 1998), 58.

36   Verhey, *MG*, 136.

37   Nicholas Wade, "It's a Three Legged Race to Decipher the Human Genome," *New York Times*, 23 June 1998, F3.

[38] Nicholas Wade, "In Genome Race, Government Vows to Move up Finish," *New York Times*, 15 September 1998, F3.

[39] Nicholas Wade, "New Company Joins Race to Sequence Human Genome," *New York Times*, 18 August 1998, F6.

Being Filled with the Holy Spirit

Eldon Woodcock

On several occasions the New Testament designates people as "filled with the Holy Spirit." What does this involve? What did people do when they were filled with the Holy Spirit? How did they get that way?

The purpose of this paper is to examine the New Testament teaching on being filled with the Holy Spirit. We shall briefly survey what it means to be filled or full. We shall explore what light these concepts shed on what it means to be filled with the Holy Spirit. We shall examine what Spirit-filled people in the first century A.D. did. Then we shall consider some results of being filled with the Holy Spirit and some factors involved in becoming filled with the Holy Spirit. Finally we shall mention insights on the topic by some early Alliance leaders.

I. What It Means to Be Filled

A. The terms and their basic meanings

In New Testament Greek only two words with their cognates that mean to fill, to fulfill, to complete are used in association with the Holy Spirit: *pleroo* and *pimplemi*.[1] Both words are flexible enough to designate several kinds of fillings.

B. Their usage in the New Testament

Both words mean to finish, complete, fulfill.[2] Both words refer to a filling with something physical, such as fish, fragrance or wine.[3] Both words describe unbelievers as filled with, i.e., characterized by, certain negative qualities (e.g., Romans 1:29).[4]

Both words picture believers as filled with, i.e., characterized by, certain positive qualities.[5]

75

The verb *pleroo* described Christians as "full of goodness" and "complete in knowledge" ("full of all knowledge," ASV) and thus "competent to instruct one another" (Romans 15:14). Paul asked God "to fill Christians with the knowledge of His will through all spiritual wisdom and understanding" in order to live God-pleasing and fruitful lives (Colossians 1:9-10). He prayed that Christians would be "filled with the fruit of righteousness that comes through Jesus Christ" (Philippians 1:11). Jesus urged His disciples to obey Him so that their joy would be complete (John 15:11). Jesus (John 17:13) and Paul (Romans 15:13) prayed that Christians would be filled with joy and peace so that they would overflow with hope by the power of the Holy Spirit. The disciples were pictured as filled with joy and the Holy Spirit (Acts 13:52). Paul was "greatly encouraged" ("full of comfort," 2 Corinthians 7:4, ASV).

The verb *pimplemi* pictured the witnesses of Jesus' healing a paralytic as "filled with awe" because of the remarkable miracle they had observed (Luke 5:26). It described a similar reaction to Peter's healing a cripple—the people "were filled with wonder and amazement at what had happened to him" (Acts 3:10).

It is important to note that these qualities characterized the people who were filled with them. This is a significant point to consider in discussing being filled with the Holy Spirit. People filled with the Holy Spirit are characterized by some of His qualities.

In spite of the brevity of the previous survey, a thorough study of the New Testament data would show that the word families associated with *pleroo* and *pimplemi* cover the same range of meanings. They appear to be virtually synonymous.[6] Thus they can plausibly be understood to convey similar meanings when referring to Spirit-filling.

II. What It Means to Be Filled with the Holy Spirit

A. Prerequisites

Every Christian has a personal relationship with the divine Person, the Holy Spirit. This is the result of several of His operations which will be mentioned briefly in order to suggest their relationship to His filling.

1. The Holy Spirit's regenerative work: Regeneration is the act by God that causes the new birth to occur, thereby imparting eternal life. It occurs simultaneously with saving faith. The New Testament describes regenerated believers as born of the Spirit and as saved through the renewal of the Holy Spirit (John 3:5; Titus 3:5). His regenerating work initiates an ongoing relationship with believers. It is the basis for His future ministries to Christians.

2. The Holy Spirit's baptizing work: There is only one New Testament text that states the nature of the Holy Spirit's baptizing work. That is Paul's statement: "For we were all baptized by one Spirit into one body" (1 Corinthians 12:13a). The aorist tense of *baptizo* and the words, "we all," clearly label this baptism as a past event involving all Christians. Since it has already happened to all Christians, it evidently occurred at their conversion. The passive voice of *baptizo* and the instrumental dative (*en eni pneumati*, "by one spirit") identify the Holy Spirit as the One who caused this event to occur. The phrase, *eis en soma*, "into one body," indicates the result of this baptism.

For Paul, baptism by the Holy Spirit involves His placing new believers into the body of which Jesus Christ is the Head (Ephesians 5:23). This is doubtless the occasion for His defining each member's function within the body of Christ by the distribution of spiritual gifts (Romans 12:3-8; 1 Corinthians 12:5-31). This baptism, also designated as being baptized into Christ, brings new believers into union with Christ in His death and resurrection (Romans 6:1-10; Galatians 3:27), for they are members of His body.

By its effect of placing new believers into the body of Christ, baptism by the Holy Spirit puts them into a position that enables them to access spiritual power. But it does not, in itself, activate that power. Only members of the body of Christ have the benefit of the Holy Spirit's other ministries to believers.

3. The Holy Spirit's indwelling of Christians:[7] Since the Holy Spirit's indwelling is a benefit of being justified by faith in Jesus Christ, He lives within all who have been justified (Romans 5:5). His presence is a gift to Christians received at the time of their conversion (1 Corinthians 2:12; 2 Corinthians 5:5). Thus the Holy Spirit lives within all Christians and only in them (Romans 8:9; Galatians 4:6). In fact, anyone who lacks His presence is unsaved (Romans 8:9; Jude 19).

Paul pictured Christians as the temple of the Holy Spirit, a vivid image of His living within them (1 Corinthians 3:16; 6:19-20 cf. Ephesians 2:19-22). As the dwelling place of the Holy Spirit, the temple is holy because He is holy. Thus Christians, inhabited by the Holy Spirit, are also to be holy.

The indwelling Holy Spirit brings God's presence into the lives of believers. It is through the indwelling Holy Spirit that God applies the power that produces life (i.e., spiritual vitality) within Christians, enabling them to stand firm in Christ and to develop a holy lifestyle (Romans 8:11; 2 Corinthians 1:21-22).

Only those regenerated, baptized and indwelt by the Holy Spirit are in a position to be filled with the Holy Spirit.

B. The Holy Spirit's control

There is an analogy between being filled with a quality or feeling and being filled with the Person of the Holy Spirit.[8] When described as filled, a person is dominated or characterized by the quality or Person that does the filling.

To be filled with the Holy Spirit involves an expansion and intensification of the impact of His indwelling presence. It is to have His presence saturate one's being with His qualities of godliness in life and power in ministry. To be filled with the Holy Spirit is for Him to advance His presence and power within one to the full extent that He desires.[9] It is for Him to take possession of the believer's mind, thereby controlling his disposition and guiding him.[10] By means of this controlling influence, the Holy Spirit "*moves* the one who is filled into a new course of action and produces a new kind of life."[11]

C. The believer's yieldedness

What the Holy Spirit accomplishes within a believer does not depend upon how much of the Holy Spirit a believer has received. Since every believer has received the Person of the Holy Spirit who lives within him and relates to him, no believer has received only a portion of the Holy Spirit, for He is indivisible.

What the Holy Spirit accomplishes within a believer depends upon how much of the believer He controls, i.e., the extent to which the believer is yielded to His influence.[12] Since the extent of a believer's yieldedness varies, the extent of the Holy Spirit's control also varies. This is the basis for Pache's conclusion that God desires to increasingly possess more of us (i.e., of each believer).[13] As we surrender more control to the Holy Spirit, we experience spiritual growth and progressive victory over sin.[14] To maximize the Holy Spirit's influence, believers need to be completely open to His leading.[15]

J.D. Pentecost observed:

> When the apostle talks about being filled with the Spirit, he proceeds to show that one who is under the control of, or the influence of, the Holy Spirit, will

find that the controlling Holy Spirit produces an entirely different kind of life. The man is different, not because of what he is himself, but because of the power to which he has submitted himself and the Person to whom he has yielded control.[16]

There are two aspects of being filled with the Holy Spirit: (1) His personal guidance and provision of power, and (2) the believer's response of complete openness and yieldedness to His leading. These indicate the divine and human factors in the filling.

D. Continuing condition and special empowerment

Does being filled with the Holy Spirit involve a continuing condition of yieldedness to the Holy Spirit's influence or His periodic empowering for special needs in ministry? Some have suggested that being full of the Spirit designates the former and that being filled with the Spirit depicts the latter.[17] Nevertheless, this is not always the case, for Stephen was described as full of the Holy Spirit in Acts 6:3, 5, evidently indicating this continuing condition. Yet later he was again pictured as full of the Holy Spirit in 7:55, which involved a special empowering.[18] Christians were also described as empowered in ministry by a filling of the Holy Spirit (e.g., 4:8, 31).[19] Yet the command to be filled with the Holy Spirit evidently indicates an ongoing condition (Ephesians 5:18, *plerousthe*).

The picture described here is of certain Christians being filled with the Holy Spirit as a continuing condition while intermittently empowered by Him for ministry. I would suggest that these categories are not necessarily mutually exclusive (i.e., that these fillings combine the continuing condition with the special empowering), although one may, in a given text, be more prominently in view than the other. Being full of the Holy Spirit as a continuing spiritual condition does not preclude special fillings that empower the believer for ministry or for handling especially difficult situations. Nevertheless, the special empowerments occur in the context of the ongoing spiritual condition.

III. The Command to Be Filled with the Holy Spirit

The text in which this command is found is, of course, Ephesians 5:18: "Do not get drunk on wine, which leads to debauchery. Instead, be filled with the Spirit."

A. The context

In his perceptive article, Chip Anderson well described the context for this command.

> Paul's agenda in calling attention to Christ as the center of God's redemptive activity leads to his primary concern for addressing the letter: Paul writes in order that his readers might understand and recognize their place in God's redemptive plan. He so prays (1:15ff.) and so writes concerning God's activity in placing all things under Christ's authority (1:22) in order that the church might come to understand the place they now have in this activity. He prays (3:14ff.) that God would enable the church to comprehend God's plan, power and accomplishment which works first in the church (2:1-6, 11-22) and then through the church in the world (3:10, 20-21; 5:21ff.). Paul's concluding prayer in 6:15ff. also demonstrates his agenda in that he requests their continued prayers for the furtherance of the gospel through his own proclamation.[20]

B. "Do not get drunk on wine"

Leading into the key command is a prohibition against excessive drinking of alcoholic beverages.[21] This prohibition is appropriate, because alcohol depresses the centers in the brain that affect self-control, wisdom, discrimination, judgment and the ability to assess.[22] It also produces the unpleasantness of a hangover.

Along with other sins, drunkenness is a standard feature of an unregenerate lifestyle (1 Peter 4:3).[23] Wicked drunkards will not inherit the kingdom of God (1 Corinthians 6:9-10; Galatians 5:19-21). Drunkenness is among the sins that Christians are explicitly told to avoid (Romans 13:13). Christians, as sons of the light, are to avoid getting drunk and they are to maintain self-control (1 Thessalonians 5:4-8). They are not even to associate with a drunkard who claims to be a Christian (1 Corinthians 5:11). Drunkenness is incompatible with being Spirit-filled or even with basic Christian living.[24]

C. "which is debauchery"

Drunkenness, as an example of *asotia*, is pictured as debauchery, dissipation, profligacy.[25] It also depicts the excess, wastefulness and riotous living that dissipated the wealth of the prodigal son.[26] Such overindulgence in alcoholic drink is harmful to both the drinker and to others.[27] The term, *asotia*, "is broadly descriptive of moral degeneracy, laxity, and recklessness of conduct."[28]

D. "Instead"

The syntactical structure of Ephesians 5:18 consists of two present imperatives (*methyskesthe, plerousthe*) and two instrumental datives (*oino, en pneumati*).[29] The adversative conjunction, *alla* (but, instead, nevertheless) indicates a contrast between the two imperatives.[30]

The contrast here is one element in the broader contrast mentioned in the preceding context. This broad contrast was described as between the old self and the new self (Ephesians 4:22-23), between darkness and light (5:8-14), between unwise (*asophol*) and wise (*sophol*) living (5:15-17).[31] In 5:18 the contrast is between yielding to the controlling effects of excessive alcoholic consumption and yielding to the control of the Holy Spirit.[32] Each produces its characteristic lifestyle. One might express the contrast in this way: Do not be filled with alcoholic spirits, but be filled with the Holy Spirit.[33]

E. "Be filled with the Spirit"

The verb *plerousthe* (be filled) is a present passive imperative. As an imperative, it is a command that all Christians have a duty to obey.[34] The verb in the present tense indicates a continuing, ongoing action or a series of repeatable actions.[35] The passive voice depicts believers as yielding to what the Holy Spirit will accomplish in and through them.[36]

Anderson observed that the texts in Ephesians (1:10, 22c-23; 3:19; 4:10, 13) in which Paul used *pleroo / pleroma* reflect one theme: "God's ultimate purpose in Christ and the relationship of the believer to that purpose."[37] Thus believers are to be filled with the Holy Spirit who operates "through the activity of the risen and exalted Christ."[38] Anderson suggested the following contextual interpretation of Ephesians 5:12-21:

> Because the days are evil, that is, an era under the influence of the spiritual forces of wickedness, believers should understand the will of the Lord, namely His intended purpose in Christ and should conduct their lives wisely, being filled with the fullness of God's Spirit, who is both working in and through the Church to declare Christ's ultimate dominion over all realms of life.[39]

Anderson went on to state:

> This indwelling Spirit brings about mission, namely, the mission which is aligned with God's intended purpose in placing all things in heaven and on earth under Christ's feet (i.e., under His authority). Therefore, being filled with the Spirit is coming under the influence of the Spirit's power, aligning one's time and energy with the plan and purpose of God, which is the summing up of all things in Christ, who is ultimately filling all things in heaven and earth, exercising His rightful authority over all realms of life.[40]

There is an analogy between the Spirit-filled Christian and the wine-filled drunkard to the extent that both make self-comfort subservient to their respective goals. John Goodwin described being filled with the Spirit as a sort of spiritual drunkenness.[41] As drunkards are often insensitive to danger, pain and even beatings, Spirit-filled people are little bothered by worldly troubles.[42]

Being filled with the Holy Spirit affects the entire range of the believer's experience. Yet it does not involve His absolute control, for Christians continue to be capable of sinning. The Holy Spirit does not remove the believer's self-control, but does enhance the use of his intelligence.[43] Nevertheless, He does exercise a powerful influence over believers whom He fills.

Being filled with the Holy Spirit includes power for wisdom, worship and ministry.[44] The Holy Spirit "*moves* the one who is filled into a new and spiritually improved lifestyle."[45] This marvelous power is accessed by yielding to the Holy Spirit as the primary controlling influence in the believer's life.

IV. Effects of Being Filled with the Holy Spirit

A. Christian character

1. Strong spiritual interests: The indwelling Holy Spirit develops Christians' spiritual interests, but it is Spirit-filled individuals who are so saturated with the Holy Spirit's presence and influence that His agenda becomes theirs, for they "have their minds set on what the Spirit desires" (Romans 8:5). This mind-set involves them in spiritual matters. As a result, they are not greatly distracted by the annoyances and difficulties brought about by the hostile environment of the world.[46]

2. Submissiveness: After urging Christians to be filled with the Holy Spirit, Paul described such people as yielding to each other in ways that produce harmony in the most basic human relationships, including those of marriage, family and employment (Ephesians. 5:21-6:9).[47] Although the indwelling Holy Spirit does affect Christian attitudes in these basic relationships, His impact upon Spirit-filled Christians substantially increases the quality of these relationships within the Christian community. Perhaps this is why Paul's exhortations concerning these relationships immediately followed his command to be filled with the Holy Spirit.

3. Fruit of the Spirit: Since Christians have the Holy Spirit living within them, they are to be led by the Spirit (Romans 8:5), to live by the Spirit (Galatians 5:16, 25) and to bear the fruit produced by the Holy Spirit (5:22-23). Since the word fruit (*karpos*) is singular, it has a collective connotation. Thus it covers the entire list of ethical qualities described as His fruit: "love, joy, peace, patience, kindness, goodness, faithfulness, gentleness and self-control" (Galatians 5:22-23). When Christians are Spirit-filled, they are controlled by the Holy Spirit who thoroughly develops and makes conspicuous these attitudes and qualities within them.[48]

B. Christian worship

1. Music: For Paul, one manifestation of being Spirit-filled was the consistent and ongoing quality of worship. He noted two aspects of the musical element in the Spirit-filled Ephesian worship. Christians were to "speak to one another with psalms, hymns and spiritual songs"; Paul also told them to "sing and make music in your heart to the Lord" (Ephesians 5:19). These two types of musical expressions covered both external and internal aspects of worship, conveying the genuine joy and priorities of Spirit-filled Christians.

2. Thankful attitude: Paul described Spirit-filled Christians as "always giving thanks to God the Father for everything, in the name of our Lord Jesus Christ" (5:20). This attitude of thanksgiving is to saturate their music.[49] To be thankful to God for everything is a refreshing contrast to the chronic complainers that permeate our population. Perhaps this is why this attitude is a consistently conspicuous quality of those who are Spirit-filled.[50] It reveals their God-centered perspective.

C. Christian ministry

Believers filled with the Holy Spirit expressed that influence in various ways. All New Testament references to people as actually filled with or full of the Holy Spirit are found in the two Lukan writings. Let us survey these texts and observe what happened when people were filled with the Holy Spirit.

1. Before Pentecost: In three texts Luke used *pimplemi* to picture ministries prior to the Lord Jesus Christ's birth. Elizabeth, filled with the Holy Spirit, uttered a prophecy concerning the virgin Mary and her Baby (Luke 1:41-45). Zechariah the priest, filled with the Holy Spirit, prophesied concerning the prophetic ministry of his son, John the Baptist (1:67-79). An angel informed Zechariah that John the Baptist would be filled with the Holy Spirit from birth, enabling him to have his prophetic ministry that would turn people to the Lord (1:15-17).

Jesus, full (*pleres*) of the Holy Spirit, was led by the Spirit into the desert for His confrontation with the devil (4:1-13).

2. Supernatural events leading to conversions:

> **a. Speaking in tongues:** On the day of Pentecost the disciples were filled with the Holy Spirit, who enabled them to speak in other tongues (Acts 2:4).[51] They declared the wonders of God in several languages (2:8-11). This led to Peter's Pentecost sermon (2:14-40) that resulted in about 3,000 conversions (2:41), clearly another manifestation of the Holy Spirit's power.[52]

> **b. Miracles:** Early Christians were told to select seven men to take over the apostolic task of distributing food to the poor within their church (6:1-4). To handle the disputes that had developed within this ministry, these men had to be full of the Spirit and of wisdom (6:3).[53] One of these men, Stephen, was described as full of the Holy Spirit and of faith (6:5).[54] The Holy Spirit displayed His power through these men, producing a rapidly growing number of disciples in Jeru-

salem including many priests (6:7). As a result of being full of the Holy Spirit, Stephen was also pictured as full of God's grace and power, enabling him to enhance his ministry by doing great wonders and miraculous signs among the people (6:8).[55] Although not explicitly stated here, the pattern in the Book of Acts was often for miraculous signs and effective evangelism to occur in conjunction with each other. Alarmed, the Jews developed powerful opposition, but were unable to overcome the wisdom of the Spirit-filled Stephen (6:9-10).

c. A heavenly vision: After being brought to trial on trumped-up charges of blasphemy (6:11-14), Stephen presented an impassioned summary of Hebrew history that did more to condemn and enrage the Sanhedrin than to aid his defense (7:2-53). Then, full of the Holy Spirit, Stephen "looked up to heaven and saw the glory of God, and Jesus standing at the right hand of God" (7:55).[56] Still full of the Holy Spirit, Stephen, even as he was dying, interceded for his enemies, asking God not to hold their sin against them (7:60).[57] Although Saul witnessed and approved these events at the time (8:1), he was later converted. Stephen's martyrdom may have been a factor in preparing him for that change.

Ananias prayed for Saul to regain his sight and to be filled with the Holy Spirit, a necessity for his apostolic ministry of healing and evangelism (9:17).[58] Paul was immediately healed of his divinely induced blindness (9:18). Nothing more was stated then about his being filled with the Holy Spirit.

Later, however, Paul was described as filled with the Holy Spirit (13:9).[59] On that occasion he pronounced a curse of blindness upon Elymas, a Jewish magician and false prophet (13:4-11). As a result, the proconsul of Cyprus was converted (13:12).

3. Evangelism: Peter's healing of a cripple provided him with another opportunity to preach the gospel (3:1-26). As a result, the total number of men who believed in the Lord Jesus Christ grew to about 5,000 (4:4). Jewish opposition brought about the arrest of Peter and John who had to defend themselves before the Jewish authorities (4:1-7). On this occasion Peter, filled with the Holy Spirit, preached the gospel to the hostile Jewish leaders (4:8-12).[60] Although there was no indication of any conversion occurring then, the text noted the Jewish concern about the continuing spread of the gospel among the people (4:17).

With the Jewish opposition against their evangelism increasing, the Christians gathered together to pray specifically for boldness in their presenting God's Word and for God's healing and miraculous power to be activated (4:23-30). God answered their prayer by filling them with the Holy Spirit, thereby providing His means of fulfilling both requests (4:31).[61] As a result, they did speak the word of God boldly and continued their healing ministry (4:31; 5:12). As Schippers observed, "The filling is not an end in itself, but the condition for speaking with boldness in the missionary situation."[62]

The church in Antioch had a thriving evangelistic ministry, even extending their outreach to Gentiles—with many people believing and turning to the Lord (11:19-21). Sent from Jerusalem to investigate the situation, Barnabas approved and encouraged them to be true to the Lord (11:22-23). In this context, Barnabas was described as "full of the Holy Spirit and faith" (11:24).[63] Again the text states that many people were brought to the Lord (11:24). As a man full of the Holy Spirit, Barnabas clearly supported and doubtless participated in their outreach. His being full of the Holy Spirit may also have produced his gracious and generous character that prompted him to bring Paul to minister to the church at Antioch (11:25-26), and to sell his land to produce funds for distribution to the Christian poor (4:32-37).

During his first missionary journey Paul preached the gospel at Pisidian Antioch (13:1-47). His message was generally rejected by the Jews, but among the Gentiles "all who were appointed for eternal life believed" (13:48). Furthermore, "the word of the Lord spread through the whole region" (13:49). Jewish opposition managed to expel Paul and Barnabas from the region (13:50-51). Nevertheless, the Christians "were filled with joy and with the Holy Spirit" (13:52).[64] Their fullness was evidently linked to their ministry, both previously in Pisidian Antioch and following in Iconium (14:1-7).

D. Summary of the New Testament data

Our survey of the New Testament data leads us to three conclusions.

1. Manifestations of being Spirit-filled were quite varied. The Book of Acts describes Spirit-filled people as speaking in tongues, performing miracles, proclaiming the gospel and being gracious. Yet they did not necessarily do all of these things at any given time. Nor did any one of these occur every time someone was described as filled with the Holy Spirit. This means that there is no one manifestation that must occur every time that one is filled with the Holy Spirit. Being filled with the Holy Spirit thus cannot be limited to only one manifestation.

2. Being filled with the Holy Spirit is closely connected to ministry—especially proclaiming the Word of God. At no time after Pentecost are Christians pictured as seeking or praying to be filled with the Holy Spirit. Rather, they were filled with the Holy Spirit in connection with their ministry—especially that of evangelism. Any spiritual power involved in this filling was bestowed in a context of and for the purpose of Christian service. Thus an important aspect of being filled with the Holy Spirit is a divine empowering for a specific situation in a specific ministry. As such, it will not necessarily be permanent.

3. The terms designating being filled with the Holy Spirit convey the same meaning. When associated with the Holy Spirit, the usage of *pleroo* and *pomplemi* indicates that these words and their cognates have the same range of meanings. They are virtually equivalent terms. There is thus no observable difference in meaning between *pleroo* and *pimplemi* when designating a person as filled with the Holy Spirit.[65] Nor is there any noticeable difference between being full of or filled with the Holy Spirit. These expressions are clearly and consistently connected with Christian ministries.

V. Conditions for Being Filled with the Holy Spirit

A. The lack of explicit New Testament texts

In discussions on being filled with the Holy Spirit, people invariably ask, "How do we get filled with the Holy Spirit? What are the conditions for it?" These are reasonable and practical questions.

Yet, curiously, there is no New Testament exhortation that explicitly identifies a condition for being filled with the Holy Spirit! The New Testament writers did not even mention a condition for that filling.

Nevertheless, the various books on the Holy Spirit present several conditions for being filled with the Holy Spirit. These include self-examination (Acts 20:28; 1 Corinthians 11:28), recognizing one's spiritual emptiness, desiring and seeking to be filled (John 7:37-39; 1 Corinthians 12:31), asking in prayer to be filled (Luke 11:13) and believing that you are filled (Romans 14:23; Galatians. 3:1-5, 14).[66] None of these New Testament texts cited is relevant to being filled with the Holy Spirit. They involve either receiving the Holy Spirit or some spiritual issue that does not directly involve the Holy Spirit at all.

In the absence of viable New Testament proof texts, one may find conditions for being filled with the Holy Spirit only by drawing some reasonable inferences. This is somewhat precarious, for it is not clear how many or what conditions we should infer. Nevertheless, here are a few suggestions.

B. Inferred conditions

1. "Do not grieve the Holy Spirit of God" (Ephesians 4:30). The Greek verb rendered "grieve" is a present active imperative form of *lupeo*. It means to grieve, wound, cause pain, produce remorse or insult.[67] The ongoing pattern of inconsistency between faith professed and contradictory actions insults God's righteousness and brings distressing pain to Him.[68] Especially grievous to God is the behavior mentioned in the context, including falsehood (4:25), sinful anger (4:26), stealing (4:28), unwholesome conversation (4:29), bitterness, rage, brawling, slander and every form of malice (4:31)—sins that disrupt the fellowship of the church.[69]

What grieves the Holy Spirit must be broader than what is mentioned in the context; the presence of *any* sin grieves Him, since it is contrary to His holy nature.[70] Since the Holy Spirit finds it necessary to convict the Christian of his sin and press him to deal with it, He will not fill him until that has been done.[71] The remedy to grieving the Holy Spirit and suffering the disruption of His fellowship is for the Christian to confess his sins and be cleansed by Jesus Christ (1 John 1:9). The more the Christian appreciates that cleansing and the more he loves God, the more strongly motivated he will be to avoid grieving the Holy Spirit.[72]

2. Do not put out the Spirit's fire (1 Thessalonians 5:19). The Greek verb translated "put out the fire" is a present active imperative form of *sbennumi*. It is evidently equivalent to an order to stop doing what they were doing.[73] Literally, *sbennumi* means to extinguish a fire, but in its figurative sense it means to quench, stifle, suppress.[74]

In the context it is prophecy as an expression of the Holy Spirit's activity that is not to be contemptuously suppressed.[75] Yet the principle of quenching the Holy Spirit was not limited to prophecy.[76] More broadly, it involves resisting His will, inevitably stifling His guiding influence.[77] Such resistance severely hampers His filling, since a basic quality of being filled with the Holy Spirit is being controlled by Him. The exhortation not to put out the Spirit's fire is to yield to His guiding influence, following His lead (Romans 8:14).[78]

The relationship between grieving and quenching the Holy Spirit is not entirely clear.[79] The Spirit is grieved by sinful behavior that violates His holy standard and thus brings Him pain. His fire is put out or quenched by resistance to His will that hinders His influence. The one involves issues of morality; the other, issues of guidance. Yet there may be some overlap in these categories that prevents making an absolute distinction. In both exhortations the key response for the believer is to yield to the Holy Spirit and follow His leading.

3. "Live by the Spirit" (Galatians 5:16). The verb, *peripateite*, is a present active imperative, picturing continuous action. Meaning "to walk," it often conveys the figurative idea, "to live."[80]

By its very nature walking involves dependence upon the strength of one's legs and the strength of the surface to hold one's weight. Similarly, walking or living by the Spirit involves one's dependence upon the presence and power of the Holy Spirit who lives within.[81] Believers need the enabling power of the Holy Spirit in order to follow the path that God has set for them—in both their lives and ministries.

4. Be involved in ministry. Our survey of the New Testament data on being filled with the Holy Spirit made clear its close relationship to ministry, for virtually every reference to that filling occurred in a context of ministry—often evangelism. Spirit-filling was thus not intended to produce a special spiritual status. Rather, it was a divine equipping for service.

5. What is the place of these inferred conditions? It is not entirely clear whether these are conditions for or results of being filled with the Holy Spirit. Strong spiritual interests, a holy lifestyle, the fruit of the Holy Spirit, submissiveness to God and involvement in ministry have been previously mentioned as results of being filled with the Holy Spirit.

Which comes first—the Holy Spirit's working within the believer or the believer's turning to Him? Is the believer's yieldedness to the Holy Spirit in the spiritual and moral realms the result of His working or a condition for it? Is the believer's involvement in Christian ministry the result of being filled with the Holy Spirit or a condition for it?

Paradoxically, both may be involved, for they may involve a symbiotic relationship in which the Spirit's working and the believer's yieldedness are linked by a two-directional flow.

Thus the Spirit's initiative and the believer's response are both involved. These inferred conditions may define the nature of the desired response by believers, but they will not occur without the Holy Spirit's involvement. What the Holy Spirit achieves will be limited by the believer's response.

This would seem to leave the question of conditions for being filled with the Holy Spirit in a sort of limbo that is less than satisfactory. Yet we have ventured beyond explicit New Testament statements, for the New Testament does not even state that there are such conditions. It simply leaves us with its descriptions of people filled with the Spirit and the command to us to be so filled.

VI. Being Filled with the Holy Spirit in Early Alliance Literature, with Special Attention on A.B. Simpson

The teaching of early Alliance leaders on this topic was generally similar to what has just been presented. Their terminology, however, was somewhat different, for Simpson was more concerned with the content of the experience of being filled with the Holy Spirit than with developing a precise theological terminology to describe it.[82]

Like some of his contemporaries, Simpson recognized that the provisions for holiness and empowering were the results of Christ's completed work.[83] These provisions included sanctification and the baptism of the Holy Spirit.[84]

The relationships among receiving the Holy Spirit, the indwelling of the Holy Spirit, the baptism of the Holy Spirit and being filled with the Holy Spirit are not entirely clear in early Alliance literature. At times these terms are used almost interchangeably; at other times subtle distinctions among them were recognized.

Simpson described the baptism of the Holy Spirit as "the coming of the Holy Ghost personally to abide in the heart forever" and as "a definite experience in which we receive the Spirit Himself."[85] Thus, for Simpson, it is the baptism or receiving of the Holy Spirit that begins His indwelling of Christians. Yet he also understood the baptism of the

Holy Spirit to refer to subsequent fillings with the Spirit after one's initial reception of Him.[86]

For Simpson, there is a difference between having the Spirit within and being filled with the Spirit. The Holy Spirit lives within every regenerate person. Yet it is very different for the Christian who yields to Him, surrendering his life to His control.[87] Being filled involves a substantial increase in the Holy Spirit's influence.

Yet he also considered the baptism of the Holy Spirit to involve this complete surrender, thereby entering into God's full provision for holy living.[88] In connection with the Holy Spirit, Simpson used baptism and filling as virtually synonymous terms.[89] Although I believe that there is a sound exegetical basis for distinguishing between these terms, in that they picture different operations of the Holy Spirit, I find that my understanding of what is involved in being filled with the Holy Spirit is not significantly different from Simpson's—only I would not describe that filling as a baptism.

Harry L. Turner, president of The Christian and Missionary Alliance from 1954 to 1960, observed that Paul's command to be filled with the Holy Spirit indicated that Christians have a responsibility to be so filled (Ephesians 5:18). He also noted that the passive voice pointed to the Holy Spirit as the One who will do it.[90] My conclusions are similar.

Simpson understood being filled (or baptized) with the Holy Spirit as an empowering especially for producing a holy lifestyle. He perceived it as providing power not merely for service, but "for personal holiness and life."[91] Simpson wrote:

> It is primarily power for service, but it is power to receive the life of Christ; power to be, rather than to say and to do. Our service and testimony will be the outcome of our life and experience. Our works and words must spring from our inmost being, or they will have little power or efficacy.[92]

In the 1906 Conference for Prayer and Counsel Respecting Uniformity in the Testimony and Teaching of the Alliance, Simpson and his associates listed the following as the results of the baptism of the Holy Spirit: power for service, personal holiness, victory over the world and sin, the indwelling of Christ, sanctification, growth in grace and the deeper filling of the Holy Spirit.[93] Most of these items relate to the Christian's life in Christ, especially its spiritual aspects.

Simpson and his colleagues also recognized power for service as an important consequence of being filled with the Holy Spirit.[94] Yet their "not merely power for service" suggests that they rejected a merely utilitarian view of that power which enabled them to do great things in ministry.[95] Simpson understood that "what believers did flowed from their inner character."[96] Thus their holiness of life is essential for their effectiveness in service. For him, this power comes directly from the Holy Spirit who enables the yielded Christian to achieve God's purposes.[97]

Turner also surveyed the references in Acts that described people as filled with the Holy Spirit, noting how this filling affected their ministries.[98] He suggested that on those occasions when Spirit-filled people spoke in tongues, it is not clear whether all of them did (Acts 2:4; 10:44-47; 19:5-7).[99] He also suggested that when people were described as filled or full of the Holy Spirit on two or more occasions, it is not clear whether these were additional fillings or additional manifestations of the original filling.[100] (Acts 4:8, 31; 6:5; 7:55; 11:24; 13:52). Turner also suggested that there were many more Christians filled with the Holy Spirit than those specifically mentioned in the Book of Acts.[101]

Turner correctly concluded that there is no one manifestation that necessarily occurs with every filling with the Holy Spirit.[102] For him, to demand one single universal manifestation that occurs every time is to doubt God.[103] He rightly noted that the primary manifestation of being filled with the Holy Spirit is "intensified missionary zeal and power."[104]

Simpson presented several conditions for being filled with the Holy Spirit which I have summarized in five statements:[105]

> 1. Aware of the need to be emptied of self and of the world, one needs to thirst for being filled with the Holy Spirit. More than willingness, it involves a deep desire.

> 2. One needs to be aware of God's promised provision of empowering the redeemed for holiness of life and service.

> 3. One is to yield completely to God, surrendering to His control for His purposes.

> 4. One is to wait in prayer, asking for and receiving the requested filling.

5. One needs appropriating faith, trusting God to have provided what we have requested as He has promised.

Simpson's conditions for being filled with the Holy Spirit are not connected to any New Testament text directly dealing with this matter. The texts that he did mention involved either receiving the Holy Spirit or some other spiritual matter not directly related to filling.[106]

My problem with his conditions is the same as my problem with the conditions that I suggested. In the absence of explicit statements on this matter in the New Testament, both sets of conditions involve sets of inferences. Although partially different from mine, Simpson's conditions are not unreasonable. Nevertheless, in the absence of relevant New Testament data, neither he nor I can prove that one set of conditions is preferable to the other.

My conclusions on the importance and need for being filled with the Holy Spirit are similar to those of Simpson and his associates. Simpson did place more emphasis on how this filling results in holiness of life, while I stressed more the resulting power for ministry. Nevertheless, my discussion included the theme of holiness while Simpson and Turner recognized the result of power for service. If there is a slight difference, it is one of emphasis rather than substance.

VII. Conclusion

We briefly surveyed the usage of *pleroo* and *pimplemi*, two virtually synonymous Greek words that mean "to fill." When filled by a quality, one is characterized by that quality. We mentioned two Pauline texts that speak of the fullness of God or the fullness of Christ.

We have found that being filled with the Holy Spirit involves a controlling influence by the Holy Spirit over the believer and the believer's yieldedness to the Holy Spirit. This filling is both an ongoing condition and a series of special empowerments.

The two commands of Ephesians 5:18 contrasted the prohibition of drunkenness with the exhortation to be filled with the Holy Spirit. The latter is part of the Christian's responsibility which involves a continuous yielding to the Holy Spirit. It is part of God's program to fulfill His redemptive purpose through the risen and exalted Christ.

The results of being filled with the Holy Spirit include how Christians function in their character, worship and ministries. In their character they have strong spiritual interests, an attitude of submissiveness to God and bear the fruit of the Spirit. They are drawn to a more intimate relationship to God through His influence. In their worship they present God-centered musical communications to Him and to each other. They also express continually an attitude of thanksgiving to God for everything. In their ministries Spirit-filled Christians in the New Testament period spoke in tongues, miraculously healed people, saw a vision of God's glory, and on one occasion, Paul pronounced a curse of blindness. In each case these astonishing events led to conversions. Manifestations of being Spirit-filled were varied, but were especially often associated with ministry. The most frequently cited ministry for Spirit-filled Christians was evangelism.

There are no explicit New Testament texts stating any conditions for being filled with the Holy Spirit. Nevertheless, four inferred conditions were discussed: (1) Do not grieve the Holy Spirit; (2) Do not put out the Spirit's fire; (3) Live by the Spirit; (4) Be involved in ministry.

Since these are also results of being filled with the Holy Spirit, it is not clear whether they should be considered effects of or conditions for that filling. There may well be a symbiotic relationship between them with a two-directional flow.

Nevertheless, the New Testament does teach that Christians are filled and should continue to be filled with the Holy Spirit.

We surveyed the theme of being filled with the Holy Spirit in some early Alliance literature, especially Simpson. We found that my conclusions were generally consistent with theirs.[107]

In view of some looseness in the handling of pneumatological terminology in early Alliance literature, there are some variations in how the Holy Spirit's reception, baptism and filling were understood. Although my handling of these terms is more precise, I share their recognition of the primary significance of being filled with the Holy Spirit in providing power for both holiness of life and effective ministry.

Endnotes

[1]   R. Schippers, "Fullness: *Pleroo*," in *The New International Dictionary of New Testament Theology* (3 vols.), ed. Colin Brown, translated, with additions and revisions, from *Theologisches Begriffslexikon zum Neuen Testament*, ed. Lothar Coenen, Erich Beyreuther, and Hans Bietenhard (Grand Rapids, MI: Zondervan, 1975), vol. 1, 733-741, hereafter cited as *NIDNTT*. Gerhard Delling, "*Pimplemi, Empimplemi*," in *Theological Dictionary of the New Testament*, ed. Gerhard Kittel, trans. Geoffrey W. Bromiley (Grand Rapids, MI: Eerdmans, 1968), 6, 128-131; Gerhard Delling, "*pleres*," 6, 283-311, hereafter cited as *TDNT*.

[2] Both words indicate the completion of a task or a period of time (e.g. Acts 12:25; Luke 1:23). The verb, *pleroo* depicts the fulfillment of the righteous requirements of the Law (e.g. Romans 8:4). Both words picture the fulfillment of prophecy (e.g., Matthew 2:15; Luke 21:22).

[3] The verb, *pleroo*, pictures a net as filled with fish (Matthew 13:48) and a house as filled with the fragrance of perfume (John 12:3). The verb *pimplemi* depicts boats full of fish (Luke 5:7) and a sponge filled with wine vinegar (Matthew 27:48).

[4] Both words describe unbelievers as furious ("filled with wrath," ASV) at the preaching of Paul and Jesus (Acts 19:28; Luke 4:28).

[5] Only two texts use *pleroo* to designate believers as filled with a negative quality. Satan filled Ananias' heart with the intent to lie to the Holy Spirit (Acts 5:3)—with disastrous results. Jesus observed that because He had informed His disciples that He was soon to die, they were filled with grief (John 16:6).

[6] Nevertheless, see Delling, *TDNT* 6, 130-131, for the idea of a distinction between them. For him, *pimplemi* indicates satisfaction.

[7] The New Testament also pictures God as living within Christians who are thus "the temple of the living God" (2 Corinthians 6:16). It also describes Christ in Christians as their "hope of glory" (Colossians 1:27).

[8] Paul prayed for Christians to "be filled to the measure of all the fullness of God" (Ephesians 3:19). He described a purpose of certain spiritual gifts as to enable the body of Christ to attain "to the whole measure of the fullness of Christ" (Ephesians 4:11-13). It is significant that, as with regeneration and indwelling, the terminology of fullness is applied to the Father and to the Son as well as to the Holy Spirit.

[9] John Goodwin, *A Being Filled With the Spirit* (Edinburgh: James Nichol, 1867), 11-12, hereafter cited as *BFWS*.

[10] Ronald N. Mayers, "The Infilling of the Holy Spirit," *Reformed Review* 28, Spring, 1975, 157, hereafter cited as *IHS*; Michael Green, *I Believe in the Holy Spirit* (Grand Rapids, MI: 1975), 149, hereafter cited as *BHS*.

[11] J. Dwight Pentecost, *The Divine Comforter: The Person and Work of the Holy Spirit* (Westwood, NJ: Revell, 1963), 158, hereafter cited as *DC*.

[12] John F. Walvoord, *The Holy Spirit* (Findlay, OH: Dunham. 1958), 192, hereafter cited as *HS*; Rene Pache, *The Person and Work of the Holy Spirit* (Chicago: Moody, 1954), 118, hereafter cited as *PWHS*.

[13] Pache, *PWHS*, 129.

[14] Ibid., 130-131.

[15] Goodwin, *BFWS*, 11-12.

[16] Pentecost, *DC*, 157; Similarly, Walvoord, *HS*, 192, described this filling as what the Holy Spirit accomplished in the believer who is yielded to Him.

[17] Green, *BHS* 149, 172; Leon Morris, *Spirit of the Living God* (London: Inter Varsity, 1960), 89, hereafter cited as *SLG*; Pentecost, *DC*, 156.

[18] D.M. Lloyd-Jones, *Life in the Spirit in Marriage, Home and Work: An Exposition of Ephesians 5:18-6:9* (Grand Rapids: Baker, 1974), 44-46, hereafter cited as *LSMHW*, found elements of both ideas in Acts 7:55.

[19] Here the Greek verb was a form of *pimplemi*.

20 Chip Anderson "Rethinking 'Be Filled With the Spirit': Ephesians 5:18 and the Purpose of Ephesians," *Evangelical Journal* 7 (1989), 5, hereafter cited as *EJ*.

21 Bruce, *The Epistles to the Colossians, to Philemon, and to the Ephesians New International Commentary of the New Testament* (Grand Rapids, MI: Eerdmans, 1984), 379, hereafter cited as *ECPE*, identified Proverbs 23:31a, LXX, as the source of this quoted prohibition.

22 Lloyd-Jones, *LSMHW*, 15.

23 Cleon L. Rogers, Jr., "The Dionysian Background of Ephesians 5:18," *Bibliotheca Sacra* 136 (1979), 249-257, hereafter cited as *BS*, argued that the background for Ephesians 5:18 was the cult of Dionysius or Bacchus, the god of wine. Since this cult was widespread, it is possible that it had participants in Ephesus. Nevertheless, as Andrew T. Lincoln, *Word Biblical Commentary: Ephesians*, (Waco, TX: Word, 1990), 343, hereafter cited *WBCE*, pointed out, this is unlikely, for there is no evidence of any such misbehavior within the Ephesian church (as there was in Corinth). Drunkenness in Ephesus may be plausibly understood as another example of a problem that has plagued many societies.

24 Goodwin, *BFWS*, 23; Dennis Leggett, "Be Filled With the Spirit, Ephesians 5:18," *Paraclete* 23, Fall (1989), 10-11, hereafter cited as *P*.

25 Bauer, Arndt and Gingrich, *A Greek-English Lexicon of the New Testament and Other Early Christian Literature* (Chicago: University of Chicago Press, 1957), 119, hereafter cited as *GELNTOECL*.

26 Mayers, *IHS*, 158. Bruce, *ECPE*, 379, noted that the cognate adverb, *asotos* pictured the lifestyle of the prodigal son in Luke 15:13. So also Lincoln, *WBCE*, 344.

27 Bruce, *ECPE*, 379.

28 Herbert G. Miller, *Commentary on St. Paul's Epistle to the Ephesians* (London: Skeffington and Son, 1899), 281, hereafter cited as *CSPEE*.

29 Rogers, *BS*, 256.

30 Bauer, Arndt and Gingrich, *GELNTOECL*, 37.

31 Lincoln, *WBCE*, 343.

32 Pentecost, *DC* 159; Charles C. Ryrie, *The Holy Spirit*, (Chicago: Moody, 1965), 93-94, hereafter cited as *HS*.

33 Rogers, *BS*, 256, argued that since being filled with the Holy Spirit involved a supernatural filling, it would be logical to infer a supernatural filling of the wine god, Bacchus, through drinking wine. Nevertheless, the evidence does not require us to be that explicit. See Lincoln, *WBCE*, 343.

34 Goodwin, *BFWS*, 15; Mayers, *IHS*, 157.

35 Mayers, *IHS*, 344.

36 Mayers, *IHS*, 157; Anderson, *EJ*, 62, renders it, "Let yourselves be filled. . . ."

37 Anderson, *EJ*, 63.

38 Ibid.

39 Ibid.

40 Ibid., 64.

[41] Goodwin, *BFWS*, 233-234. Lincoln, *WBCE*, 344 cited Philo (*De Ebr.*, 146-148) as making a similar analogy between the characteristics of drunkenness and being possessed by God. Lincoln also noted the confusion between Spirit-filled people at Pentecost with drunks (Acts 2:4, 13, 15).

[42] Goodwin, *BFWS*, 233-234, thoroughly developed this intriguing analogy, probably more than is warranted, for there is a significant difference between enslavement of a habit-forming drug and conscious yielding to the Holy Spirit's influence. Furthermore, part of the fruit of the Holy Spirit (Galatians 5:22-23) is self-control, a quality that the drunkard lacks. Nevertheless, that there is some validity in this analogy is indicated by Paul's contrast.

[43] Bruce, *ECPE*, 380.

[44] Lincoln, *WBCE*, 345.

[45] Pentecost, *DC*, 158.

[46] Goodwin, *BFWS*, 233-234. See my prior discussion of an analogy between the Spirit-filled Christian and the wine-filled drunkard.

[47] Ryrie, *HS*, 102.

[48] Tim La Haye, *Spirit-Controlled Temperament* (Wheaton, IL: Tyndale House, 1966), 58, hereafter cited as *SCT*; Wick Broomall, *The Holy Spirit: A Scriptural Study of His Person and Work* (New York: American Tract Society, 1940), 181-183.

[49] The exhortation to express thanksgiving in music was even more clearly stated in Colossians 3:16-17.

[50] Pache, *PWHS*, 134.

[51] The Greek word translated "filled" is *ekplesthesan*, from *pimplemi*.

[52] LaHaye, *SCT*, 60.

[53] The Greek word translated "full" is *plereis*.

[54] *Plere.*

[55] *Pleres.*

[56] Ibid.

[57] Pache, *PWHS*, 134.

[58] *Plesthes* from *pimplemi*.

[59] *Plestheis* from *pimplemi*.

[60] Ibid.

[61] *Eplesthesan* from *pimplemi*.

[62] Schippers, *NIDNTT*, 739.

[63] *Pleres.*

[64] *Eplerounto.*

[65] Lukan texts describing the charismatic power of Spirit-filled people in ministry often use a form of *pimplemi*. (Acts 2:4, 4:8, 31, 9:17; 13:9). Nevertheless, this aspect is not absent from the *pleroo* family, for these terms picture Stephen as full of the Spirit in the context of a charismatically powerful ministry of evangelism and miraculous signs (Acts 6:3-8) and as seeing a revelatory vision of the ascended Christ that

prompted him to pray for his enemies to be forgiven even as they were killing him (Acts 7:55). They also depict Barnabas and the disciples as full or filled with the Holy Spirit in a context of evangelistic ministry (Acts 11:24; 13:52).

66 e.g., LaHaye, *SCT*, 63, 66; Mayers, *IHS*, 161; Pache, *PWHS*, 120.

67 James F. Holladay, Jr., "Ephesians 4:30: Do Not Grieve the Spirit," *Review and Expositor* 94 (1997), 84, hereafter cited as *EDNGHS*; Bauer, Arndt and Gingrich, *GELNTOECL*, 482-483.

68 Holladay, *EDNGHS*, 84.

69 Ibid., 85.

70 Walvoord, *HS*, 200.

71 Pentecost, *DC*, 159; Goodwin, *BFWS*, 19, suggested that the grieving of the Holy Spirit will diminish His activity within Christians much as grief diminishes human energy. His relative inactivity produces spiritual deadness (Goodwin, 269).

72 Halladay, *EDNGHS*, 86.

73 Leon Morris, *The First and Second Epistles to the Thessalonians, New International Commentary on the New Testament* (Grand Rapids, MI: Eerdmans, 1959), 175-176, hereafter cited as *FSET*; Ryrie, *HS*, 95; But see F.F. Bruce, *Word Biblical Commentary: 1 & 2 Thessalonians* (Waco, TX: Word, 1982), 125, hereafter cited as *WBCT*, for the view that it means to habitually avoid doing this—not to stop doing it.

74 Bauer, Arndt and Gingrich, *GELNTOECL*, 752.

75 Bruce, *WBCT*, 125; Goodwin *BFWS*, 279.

76 Morris, *FSET*, 175.

77 Walvoord, *HS*, 197.

78 Ibid., 199.

79 Morris, *SLG*, 98, does not consider quenching to differ much from grieving since both involve conduct contrary to the Holy Spirit's will.

80 Bauer, Arndt and Gingrich, *GELNTOECL*, 654-655, describes it as referring figuratively to the "walk of life."

81 Walvoord, *HS*, 204; cf. Goodwin, *BFWS*, 257.

82 Richard Gilbertson, *The Baptism of the Holy Spirit* (Camp Hill, PA: Christian Publications, Inc., 1993), 117.

83 Ibid., 77ff.

84 Ibid.

85 A.B. Simpson, "The Baptism with the Spirit," *The Christian Alliance and Missionary Weekly* (30 Sept., 1892), 120; "Phases and Phrases of the Deeper Life, *Living Truths* (Oct., 1902), 181. Both quotations were cited in Gilbertson, *The Baptism of the Holy Spirit*.

86 Gilbertson, *The Baptism of the Holy Spirit*, 117.

87 Leona Frances Choy, "Albert Benjamin Simpson" in *Powerlines: What Great Evangelicals Believed about the Holy Spirit*, 1850-1930 (Camp Hill, PA: Christian Publications, 1990), 237.

[88] Gilbertson, *The Baptism of the Holy Spirit*, 103.

[89] Ibid., 116. Harry L. Turner, *The Voice of the Spirit* (Harrisburg, PA: Christian Publications, Inc., n.d.), 137. Turner considered baptism of the Spirit and filling with the Spirit to be two distinct doctrines, but did not state what the distinction is. He was more concerned with the Holy Spirit's impact than the terms describing it.

[90] Turner, *The Voice of the Spirit*, 132-133.

[91] Gilbertson, *The Baptism of the Holy Spirit*, 55.

[92] Ibid., 104-105. Here Simpson's listing a deeper filling of the Holy Spirit as a result of His baptism indicates a distinction between filling and baptism. Yet it is not clear what that distinction is. Nevertheless, the characteristics and effects of both appear to be the same in Simpson's thought. Simpson, *The Holy Spirit*, vol. 2, 95-96, also included joy and the fruit of the Spirit (Galatians 5:21-22).

[93] A.B. Simpson, *The Holy Spirit or Power From on High* Vol. 2 (Harrisburg, PA: Christian Publications, Inc., 1896), 79.

[94] Ibid., 89, described one of the functions of the Holy Spirit's power is to enable Christians to render effective service.

[95] Gilbertson, *The Baptism of the Holy Spirit*, 127.

[96] Ibid.

[97] Ibid., 127-128.

[98] Turner, *The Voice of the Spirit*, 122-130.

[99] Ibid., 127, 129, 130. Although these texts are not quite explicit on this point, they do convey the impression that all of those who were filled with the Holy Spirit on those three specific occasions did speak in tongues.

[100] Ibid., 127, 129. Although none of these texts is explicit on this point, the statement that one was filled with the Holy Spirit on a specific occasion implies a new and fresh filling (Acts 4:8, 31; 13:52). The references to people as full of the Holy Spirit on various occasions (Acts 6:5; 7:55; 11:24) are less clear. Nevertheless, I am inclined to interpret them the same way.

[101] Ibid., 123-124. Although plausible, his conclusion provides no data for our guidance.

[102] Ibid., 140, 142.

[103] Ibid., 140.

[104] Ibid., 142-144. See also Choy, *Powerlines*, 260.

[105] A.B. Simpson, "Filled with the Spirit," reprinted in *The Best of A.B. Simpson*, compiled by Keith M. Bailey (Camp Hill, PA: Christian Publications, Inc., 1987), 41-45; Gilbertson, *The Baptism of the Holy Spirit*, 114-115; Simpson, *The Holy Spirit*, vol. 2, 97-98.

[106] In fairness to Simpson, he did not always clearly distinguish among the Holy Spirit's reception, baptism and filling.

[107] These conclusions are also consistent with the current Alliance Statement of Faith which reads: "It is the will of God that each believer should be filled with the Holy Spirit and be sanctified wholly, being separated from sin and the world and fully dedicated to the will of God, thereby receiving power for holy living and effective service."

Contextualization:
The Continuing Search for Relevance

Richard B. Pease

I t was late August in the summer of 1963. My wife and I, along with our two small children, accompanied another missionary family to our very first church service in Japan. We made our way through the narrow, incredibly crowded streets to the little Christian and Missionary Alliance church in suburban Osaka, Japan. The small congregation greeted us with bows and awkward handshakes. We slipped off our shoes and went into Pastor Oizumi's cramped apartment, where the church met.

We sat with our legs crossed on *zabuton* cushions on the *tatami* straw mat floor. After what seemed an eternity, the service drew to a close. With considerable difficulty we unwound our legs and stood for the benediction. Following the service, we were warmly welcomed as the new missionaries. The meal consisted of *very* generous portions of raw fish on rice, which we washed down with green tea. Then we bowed, shook hands, slipped back into our shoes and returned home.

Thus began our first introduction to the intricacies of cross-cultural communication. Though we had not started language study and could not understand the message, we had recognized the hymns. Except for the offering being taken after the message, the order of worship was similar to our Alliance church back home. A few months later, the pastor moved into a single residence and the church moved as well. Now the congregation could worship more like a "real church," seated on folding chairs instead of the floor. A pump organ was purchased and the pastor preached from a pulpit instead of from a kneeling position.

We watched with great interest as the church wrestled with the question of how to establish a vibrant witness for Christ in a major urban area of Japan. We soon discovered that the issues the Osaka church struggled with were not unlike the questions being asked in other areas of the world. What is the culturally relevant way to preach, to plant churches, to do evangelism, to train leaders and to establish a theologically sound scriptural base for mission? Though the terminology would be popularized later, I came to share the conviction expressed by Dean Gilliland that "contextualization, biblically based and Holy Spirit-led, is a requirement for evangelical missions today."[1]

The ongoing discussions concerning contextualization are taking on an added urgency as the Church in America joins in the debate. Immigration has brought large numbers of people of other religions to our doorstep. While it is estimated that over sixty percent of the United States population of some 270 million are related to some form of a religious organization, more than thirty percent, or about 81 million, claim no religious affiliation.[2] Since there are only nine other nations in the world with a total population of more than 81 million, the United States is one of the greatest mission fields in the world today. Only China, India, and Indonesia have more lost people.[3]

The Alliance, like many other denominations, is experiencing significant growth in its ethnic churches. Church leaders are developing strategies at all levels to find more effective ways to evangelize unreached people groups here and overseas. Much prayer and planning are currently focused on effectively reaching major resistant blocks of people, such as the Muslim world. Contextualization must then be seen as an ongoing challenge and not just a passing fad. The fundamental issues involved are simply too important.

David Hesselgrave and Edward Rommen state the matter succinctly in their book, *Contextualization: Meanings, Methods and Models,* by noting that contextualization

> is more than a neologism, it is a necessity. Of course this thesis rests on certain presuppositions. First, it is imperative that the Great Commission be fulfilled and the world evangelized. Second, however world evangelism is defined, at the very least it entails an understandable hearing of the gospel. Third, if the gospel is to be understood, contextualization must be true to the complete authority and unadulterated message of the Bible on the one hand, and it must be related to the

cultural, linguistic, and religious background of the respondents on the other.[4]

The Apostle Paul framed the issue in First Corinthians 9:22: "I have become all things to all men so that by all possible means I might save some." Thus, while the concept of contextualization is hardly new, the terminology is of recent vintage. Until the late 1960s, the term of choice was indigenization. In the nineteenth century, two great missionary strategists, Henry Venn of the Church Missionary Society in London, and Rufus Anderson of the American Board of Commissioners for Foreign Missions, developed the famous "three-self formula."[5] Early Protestant missionaries tended to fear that any use of pagan forms and symbols would lead to syncretism. As Hiebert notes, in an attempt to avoid syncretism, "Western forms were often introduced to convey Christian meanings."[6] Generally, a Western model of the Church was imposed, sometimes with little attempt to adapt it to the local culture. Not surprisingly, the result was that nationals often associated Christianity with the West.

Anderson and Venn attempted to address the prevailing missionary methodology in their day, insisting that churches should be self-supporting, self-governing and self-propagating.[7] However, times change and the Church's response to these changes is a dynamic process.

Daniel Sanchez has noted that the "change in focus from indigenization to contextualization is one of the most significant in contemporary missiology." Indigenization comes from the word *indigenous*, which means "native to a given area." The term contextualization is derived from the word *context*, which has its roots in the Latin word *contextus*, meaning "weaving together." Sanchez says that contextualization may be understood then, in terms of "making concepts and methods relevant to a historical situation." He defines missiological contextualization as "enabling the message of God's redeeming love in Jesus Christ to become alive as it addresses the vital issues of a sociocultural context and transforms its worldview, its values, and its goals."[8]

Compared with indigenization, contextualization takes the process of cross-cultural communication of the gospel to a deeper involvement with the cultural context in missiology.[9] It focuses on the importance of culture and context. As C. Gordon Olson says, it is "a strategy which takes into account the various cultures into which God's eternal message comes and is communicated to people of diverse cultures."[10]

The 1970s are usually identified as the time when the concept of contextualization began to move onto center stage. Sanchez has noted the earlier consultations on contextualization convened in Africa, such as the 1955 conference in Ghana exploring the relationship between African culture and Christianity, followed by several other conferences.[11] In Latin America, concerns about the Church and society led to discussions focusing on doing theology in context. Gustavo Guttierez wrote *Theology of Liberation* in 1971, followed by J. Migueuz-Bonino's *Doing Theology in a Revolutionary Situation* in 1975, both illustrations of contextual theology.[12] The World Council of Churches consultations in Uppsala in 1968, followed by Bossey in 1971 addressed issues in contextualization. The Lausanne movement, beginning in 1974, dealt with crucial concerns in contextualization.[13]

Though the term contextualization has all but replaced the earlier concepts of indigenization, certain problems remain unresolved. One is the problem of definition. Hesselgrave has noted the lack of agreement as to the precise definition, pointing out the danger of an Alice-in-Wonderland approach which insists that "words mean what I say they mean."[14] A second issue is the array of models put forth to deal with contextualization. Van Engen describes Stephen Bevans' six models of contextual theology: the anthropological, translation, praxis, synthetic, semiotic and transcendental.[15] Van Engen then proceeds to present four major models of contextualization: communication, cultural relevance, liberation and interfaith dialogue, and suggests a fifth model, knowing God in context.[16] These models illustrate the wide impact contextualization is having on the contemporary church scene.

The lack of precise definition and broad application make it more difficult to evaluate and critique the movement and the methodology involved. It is probably fair to say that virtually any attempt today to formulate theology and communicate the gospel cross-culturally can legitimately be described as contextualization. David Hubbard, former president of Fuller Theological Seminary, was probably correct when he wrote, "no word in the Christian lexicon is as fraught with difficulty, danger and opportunity as contextualization."[17]

A crucial issue in the search for relevance is the extent to which the context dictates our message and methodology. The *Missio Dei* is nothing less than God's mission. But as Van Engen points out, "the *Missio Dei* happens in specific places and times in our contexts. Its content, validity, and meaning are derived from Scripture; yet its action, significance and transforming power happen in our midst."[18] Van Engen summarizes four ways that others have suggested for addressing this issue, then adds a fifth way for us to consider.

The first linkage that Van Engen describes involves a "theology from above." In the Roman Catholic Church and mainline Protestant denominations, this usually involves using church tradition as the link between the Bible and its mission. In this case, the church interprets Scripture and derives its missiological and evangelistic task from what it sees in Scripture. In this setting, "the extension of the institutional church and its agendas become the heart of mission."[19]

A second method in the "from above" category involves seeing the Bible as the source of the commands for mission in such passages as the Great Commission in Matthew 28:18-20. Van Engen identifies the basic problem with these approaches as not allowing the Scriptures themselves to interact with the present contexts of mission. He says in doing this, the Scriptures are "mediated, reduced, and filtered either by the agendas of the institutional church or by the guilt-based appeal of the one who expounds on the commands." Either way, when we put church tradition or our understanding of the commands between the Scripture and the context, we "reduce the impact that Scripture can have in transforming the way we understand, exercise and evaluate our missional action."[20]

The third and fourth models are based on doing theology "from below," where the starting point is not the Scripture, but the contextual agenda.[21] This approach has characterized churches associated with the World Council of Churches since World War II. In effect, once the agenda has been determined, the search is made for "exemplary cases" in the Bible to support their position. Van Engen then moves on to critique evangelical missions, which are engaged in ministries such as church planting, development, health, education, urban ministries, etc., and seeks to legitimatize their activities by appealing to Scripture.

While these approaches deal with contextual issues, Van Engen says that the Bible "is not allowed to critique the assumptions, motivations, or rightness of the action itself—it is used only as a justification for what has been predetermined." He also points out that "this mission is not God's. It belongs to the practitioners. The text is used primarily as a justification of the activity."

Though theology "from above" may result in irrelevance, theology "from below" carries the risk of the Church losing all sense of its prophetic role, along with being salt and light. Its desire for relevance potentially allows for the context to set the agenda. To address these problems, Van Engen advocates seeing the Bible as a "tapestry of missional themes and motifs in context."[22] This approach affirms the centrality of Scripture in missions and evangelism while acknowledging the impact of culture in communicating the message of God's Word.

This raises the question as to what people should do about their old cultural ways when they make the decision to become Christians. The interplay between culture and religious belief systems is enormously complex. In Chicago and Cairo, New York and New Delhi, Tokyo and Toronto, the questions that missionaries, pastors and those engaging in evangelism must answer are these: How does the new Christian relate his or her faith in Christ to the existing cultural beliefs and practices? Are the old ways all bad? Or are they good?

Paul Hiebert identifies three approaches to dealing with these questions. Hiebert first of all discusses denial of the old ways, which he says is rejection of contextualization. This involves rejecting most of the old customs as pagan or demonic. We do live in a fallen world where Satan has invaded all the structures of society; however, wholesale rejection of the old cultural ways leads to problems. First, it leaves a cultural vacuum that needs to be filled, and this is often done by incorporating the customs of the missionary.[23] The new missionary to Japan should not be surprised at how "Western" the Church is, since that was the model the early missionaries introduced.

A second problem in rejecting the old ways is that they merely go underground, Hiebert adds. New converts in Africa may continue to be involved in traditional celebrations, which can result in a form of Christopaganism, a blending of Christian and non-Christian practices. A third problem is that the rejection of the old ways turns the church leaders into the role of police, deciding what is right and wrong.[24]

Hiebert says a second approach is to accept the old ways, or uncritical contextualization. This also is problematic because it opens the door to serious compromise and even syncretism. It overlooks the possibility of corporate and cultural sins and minimizes the change in the lives of the converts. It can ignore the need to critically examine every facet of culture under the lens of the Word of God. While the motive to respect people and culture is admirable, the call of Scripture to growth and maturity demands that our lives be measured against the standards of God's Word.[25]

Hiebert advocates a third approach, which is critical contextualization, where "old beliefs and customs are neither rejected nor accepted without examination. They are first studied with regard to the meanings and places they have within their cultural setting and then evaluated in the light of biblical norms." He explains that this involves the leaders teaching converts the need to deal biblically with all areas of life, studying the Scripture in relation to the question under consideration.[26] These ideas have merit whether the issue is Christian young people listening to hard rock in Los Angeles, or the appropriateness of children attending Buddhist funerals in Shanghai.

The contemporary search for relevance also involves a careful examination of the current debate over the adequacy of some of the contextualization models. Louis Luzbetak, who in 1970 authored *The Church and Cultures*, in later writings suggested developing contextualization models based on translation theory. Charles Kraft built upon the work of earlier writers, suggesting that the dynamic equivalence model has certain advantages over the formal correspondence model of contextualization.[27] The formal correspondence view essentially involved a literal word-for-word translation. As Sanchez points out, it was based on the conviction that this was the most effective way of conveying the meaning and message of the Bible from one language to another.[28]

Kraft explains the concept of dynamic equivalence in translation as follows: "The informed translator endeavors to be faithful both to the original author and message and to the intended impact that the message was to have upon the original readers." Kraft contends that there is really "no such thing as an exact correspondence between a given word in one language and the most nearly corresponding word in another language." To resolve that problem, the translator seeks to produce a translation that is "true to both the message of the source documents and the normal ways of expressing such a message in the receptor language. This tends to remove the impression of stiltedness and foreignness from the translation."[29]

For better or worse, the dynamic equivalence model has had broad application in contextualization, entailing church planting, evangelistic methodologies, leadership patterns and worship styles. Essentially the question is this: What does the Church look like in another cultural context? As practitioners wrestle with cross-cultural communication of the gospel, critical contextualization becomes increasingly urgent.

Does good contextualization mean good results in ministry? Michael Pocock, a professor at Dallas Theological Seminary and president of the Evangelical Missiological Society (EMS), was quoted in an interview as saying that "one hundred percent contextualization is not going to guarantee belief."[30]

The 1997 annual meeting of EMS focused on the theme "Reaching the Resistant"; the presentations and other material were compiled into the book *Reaching the Resistant: Barriers and Bridges for Mission.* Some of the questions dealt with included: What is meant by resistant? Is resistance a result of the failure of God's people or of it not being the "fullness of time"? What degree of contextualization is legitimate?[31] Missiologists generally agree that resistance to the gospel is sometimes more related to the methodology of the messenger than to the message. In short, at least the partial answer to resistance and lack of response was and is more effective contextualization.

However, the 1997 EMS meeting challenged the assembled evangelical missiologists to consider other factors in addition to good contextualization as ways of overcoming resistance. The Church Growth Movement has used the resistance/receptivity axis as refined by Edward Dayton as a way to conceptualize the task.[32]

C. Peter Wagner says that the "first indicator of receptivity is where churches are already growing" and the second indicator is "where people are changing." These changes may be political, economic, psychological or social; they may be caused by war, internal migrations, urbanization, industrialization and many other things. However, Wagner makes an important point when he says that the "nature of the change is not as significant as the change itself."[33]

The third indicator of receptivity to the gospel is that the "masses are usually more receptive than the classes."[34] In this context, the masses refer to the ordinary working people and the poor, while the classes refer to those who are reasonably well off.

Van Engen observes that these terms, "receptive" and "resistant" have been "essentially sociological terms, descriptive of an observable phenomenon (the numerical growth of congregations), and not theological terms speaking about the spiritual state of a people group."[35] Van Engen later points out that an important missiological development that came out of the resistance/receptivity theoretical framework was the "desire for careful contextualization of the gospel in such a way that resistance could be avoided or at least lessened."[36] One assumption has been that receptivity was due, at least in part, to good contextualization; resistance was due, at least in part, to a lack of good contextualization.

Van Engen makes what may prove to be a significant contribution to the debate over resistance/receptivity by insisting that the issue be viewed far more broadly and comprehensively than good or bad contextualization. It is important to emphasize that Van Engen does not downplay the impact contextualization can have. In commenting on the resistance of the Japanese, he makes an important point:

> The insistence of the older churches in Japan on bas-
> ing their theological reflection and ministry forma-
> tion on German theology, coupled with their heavy
> use of an educational model of being a church, to-
> gether with their strong avoidance of interacting theo-
> logically with issues of Shinto shrines, holy places,
> family theology, and the world of the unseen—all of
> these have, it would seem, contributed to the sense of
> foreignness of the older churches in Japan, as seen
> through the eyes of the Japanese people. Thus, at a
> time of profound religious searching, especially on the
> part of Japanese young people, the older churches in
> Japan seem isolated and out of touch—possibly in-
> creasing resistance rather than aiding receptivity.[37]

Thus, while contextualization remains a crucial factor in effectively evangelizing Japan today, it is not the whole issue. There is more involved than fine-tuning our methodologies.

Contextualization not only involves how we communicate the gospel, it also affects our concepts of leadership in the church. To illustrate the point, it may be helpful to compare and contrast the concept of the strong leader in the American and Japanese context. C. Peter Wagner's definition provides a starting point: "Vital Sign Number One of a healthy, growing church is a pastor who is a possibility thinker and whose dynamic leadership has been used to catalyze the entire church into action for growth."[38] Such words conjure up a popular image. Edwin Hollander, in his book, *Leadership Dynamics,* says it well:

> Mention the term leadership and to most people it is
> likely to suggest an image of action and power.
> Leaders of social movements, political leaders, mili-

tary commanders, and corporate and union heads may readily spring to mind. They usually are highly visible and often have compelling personalities.[39]

In *Getting Things Done,* Lyle Schaller gives the following account of a discussion between a senior pastor and his young associate. The associate pastor had been schooled in a more democratic leadership style, and was puzzled that the senior pastor was so successful, though autocratic. In the lengthy conversation, the senior pastor made two key points. He said, "You have to recognize that we have a lot of high-powered business and professional leaders here and they expect me to be the chief executive officer." Later he says, "I am somewhat directive in my leadership approach, but I don't apologize for that. In a big church someone has to point the way, and I'm willing to do that."[40]

Even from these limited references, some key descriptive words stand out: action, power, compelling personality, high-powered, directive, dynamic, someone who points the way. Gradually, a mental image forms. We Americans begin to think of a strong leader primarily in terms of our own conceptual mapping, which becomes highly subjective. In contrast, Akio Morita, in his book, *Made in Japan,* comments on Japanese management, with special focus on Sony. He speaks of such things as developing a healthy relationship with the employees, creating a family-like feeling and developing a shared sense of fate among all employees.[41] Morita and other writers emphasize the fact that leadership in Japan is much more relationship-oriented as compared with the task-orientation of American leadership.

Japanese leadership takes into account the group consciousness so highly valued by society. The uniquely Japanese manner for reaching a consensus is called *nemawashi.* Christopher has defined it well:

> The manner in which such a consensus is achieved is known as *nemawashi,* or root-binding—a term taken from *bonsai* culture, in which, whenever a miniature tree is repotted, its roots are carefully pruned and positioned in such a way as to determine the tree's future shape. In human context, *nemawashi* involves a cautious feeling-out of all the people legitimately concerned with an issue, a highly tentative process in which no firm stands are openly taken and argument is implicit rather than explicit.[42]

110

Clearly Americans and Japanese have significant differences in leadership styles in management and business, and those differences carry over into the Church. From the perspective of contextualization, the issue is not primarily which style is superior. The consensus-based, relationship-oriented, non-directive leadership style that predominates in much of Japanese society has much to commend itself. Likewise, the task-oriented, individualistic, more highly directive style that predominates in America has value. The point of contextualization is that when cross-cultural church planting is done and church leadership trained, it is very helpful to understand the significant points of difference in how the concept of a strong leader is expressed. The American model may not work well in other cultures.

Similar points can be made when issues such as worship style, church architecture, youth programs and various outreach programs are discussed. The magnificent diversity that marks all of God's creation suggests that there may be diverse, culturally conditioned ways to express our worship to Him and how we organize ourselves into communities of believers called the Church.

The Messianic Jewish (MJ) movement represents one of the boldest attempts in recent times to contextualize. Gary Thomas, in an article in *Christianity Today*, recounts visiting Beth Yeshua in Philadelphia, a leading Messianic Jewish congregation, and asking a lady, "How long have you been a Christian?" "I'm not a Christian," the woman replied indignantly. "I'm a Messianic Jew."[43] Her rejection of the label *Christian* is but one of the many points of controversy in the MJ movement. Thomas quotes Jamie Cowen, a rabbi of Tikvat Israel, an MJ congregation based in Virginia, as saying:

> The whole thrust of Messianic Judaism is to restore the roots of the faith as a belief in Jesus as a Jewish Messiah. . . . We see our mission as being two primary things—to help Jews understand Jesus as their Messiah, and to help the Christian church understand her Jewish roots.[44]

It is not difficult to understand the desire of Jewish converts to remain Jewish. Thomas notes that the founder of Jews for Jesus, Moishe Rosen, has written:

> Jewish people often have aversions to Christian sym-
> bols such as the cross, the creche and depictions of Je-
> sus. . . . At the very least those symbols puzzle Jews,
> who have been taught from childhood not to make im-
> ages of God. At the worst, they seem to a Jewish person
> to verge on idolatry. . . . For these reasons, sometimes a
> messianic congregation can be very helpful in bridg-
> ing the culture gap between Jewish and Gentile Chris-
> tians.[45]

The efforts within the Messianic Jewish world to contextualize their
Christian faith have attracted considerable attention. It is perhaps fair
to say that the questions about not using creches, crosses and pictures of
Jesus as proper symbols of their faith have been answered to the satisfaction of many. They seem to fall within the range of Paul's formula, "To
the Jews I become like a Jew, to win the Jews" (1 Corinthians 9:20). The
continued practice of circumcision and kosher food preparation may be
more problematic if it moves in the direction of a works-based view of
salvation. Arthur Glasser is probably correct in saying that Christian
churches are very Gentile, and adding, "what the Messianic Jews are doing is not different from what the Chinese and German Christians are
doing—working hard to contextualize a faith that supersedes all nation-
alistic cultures and makes sense in their own."[46]

Recent developments in approaching the Muslim world have resulted in widespread controversy over what constitutes legitimate
methods of contextualization. At the heart of the issue is this question
on the cover of the October, 1998 issue of the *Evangelical Missions Quarterly:* "Do some approaches to Muslims cross the line into syncretism?"
The messianic mosque movement has similarities to the Jewish messianic movement. In much the same way as Jewish believers ask if they
must abandon their "Jewishness" in order to become a Christian, Muslim believers ask if they must leave their Muslim roots to follow Jesus.

The C1 to C6 spectrum has been developed as a practical tool for defining six types of "Christ-centered communities" (groups of believers
in Christ) in the Muslim world. The six Cs are essentially a categoriza-
tion for stages of contextualization within Islamic outreach and church
planting. The six Cs were formulated by a man using the pseudonym
John Travis, who has been a long-term missionary among Muslims in
Asia.[47] The six Cs may be described as:

C1—Traditional church using outsider language.

C2—Traditional church using insider language.

C3—Contextualized Christ-centered communities using insider language and religiously neutral insider cultural forms.

C4—Contextualized Christ-centered communities using insider language and biblically permissible cultural and Islamic forms.

C5—Christ-centered communities of "Messianic Muslims" who have accepted Jesus as Lord and Savior.

C6—Small Christ-centered communities of secret/underground believers.[48]

Phil Parshall, himself no stranger to controversies over contextualization in the Islamic world, warns of the slippery slide toward syncretism by some who are ministering in the Muslim world. He places C4 at high contextualization, and C5 and C6 on the syncretism end of the continuum.[49] In doing so, he joins a loud chorus of critics who raise questions about Muslim converts remaining in the mosque, reciting the Qu'ran and praying to Allah, while secretly embracing Christ.

For those of us who have had ministry experience with other non-Christian religious traditions, the messianic mosque model raises profound questions. If that model is adopted, is it not possible to move a bit farther and propose messianic temples in Buddhist countries, and messianic shrines in Japan where Shinto shrines are found in virtually every neighborhood? As Parshall draws the line in the six Cs spectrum, other attempts to contextualize must be evaluated carefully lest high contextualization drift into serious compromise and even syncretism. Conversion in the Islamic world is serious business; it may be a life or death issue in some countries. However, if the message is so compromised by attempts at contextualization, we run the risk of preaching what Paul called in Galatians 1:6-7, "a different gospel," which he then declares is "no gospel at all."

The urgent needs of our world demand our best efforts to communicate the unchanging gospel message. That message must be contextualized as we preach Christ to Hindus, Buddhists, secularists and Muslims, and it must be contextualized if the Church is going to reach New Agers, Generation Xers and others in the 81 million Americans who have no religious affiliation. Efforts at all levels need to be continually evaluated lest our user-friendly, seeker-sensitive approaches move from good contextualization toward compromise.

In conclusion, Daniel Sanchez suggests eight general principles to guide the process of contextualization which are helpful.[50] These eight principles are summarized as follows:

> 1. The Bible must be the final authority in the contextualization process. Culture and cultural items must be judged by Scripture, not Scripture by culture.
>
> 2. The supracultural elements of the gospel must be preserved in the contextualization process.
>
> 3. Local leaders need to be at the forefront in the reflection which results in contextualized theological formulations, ecclesiastical structures and evangelistic methodology.
>
> 4. Theological formulations that are developed need to be informed by previous theological reflection (e.g., dogmatic theology) and to be in dialogue with the broader Christian community to avoid heresy and syncretism.
>
> 5. Syncretism needs to be avoided in the process of local theological reflection.
>
> 6. Patience and humility need to be exercised by the broader Christian community (especially missionaries).
>
> 7. Adequate tools for an analysis of a sociocultural context need to be utilized.

8. A contextualization model that does justice both to Scripture and the sociocultural context needs to be employed.

Finally, it must be remembered that in our search for relevance, contextualization is never an end in itself. The apostle Paul said in First Corinthians 9:22, "I have become all things to all men," and then stated his purpose, "so that by all possible means I might save some." Such a lofty goal demands our best efforts to contextualize.

Endnotes

1   Dean S. Gilliland, ed., *The Word Among Us: Contextualizing Theology for Mission Today* (Dallas: Word Publishing, 1989), 3.

2   Charles Chaney, "Garden or Wilderness?: The Mission to America," in *Missiology: An Introduction to the Foundations, History, and Strategies of World Religions*, ed. Terry, Smith and Anderson (Nashville: Broadman and Holman, 1998), 243.

3   Ibid.

4   David J. Hesselgrave and Edward Rommen, *Contextualization: Meanings, Methods, and Models* (Grand Rapids: Baker Book House, 1989), xi.

5   Jonathan Lewis, ed., *World Mission: An Analysis of the World Christian Movement* (Pasadena, CA: William Carey Library, 1987), 18.

6   Paul G. Hiebert, "Form and Meaning in the Contextualization of the Gospel" in Gilliland, *The Word Among Us*, 103.

7   Lewis, *World Mission: An Analysis*, 18.

8   Daniel Sanchez, "Contextualization and the Missionary Endeavor" in *Missiology: An Introduction to the Foundation, History, and Strategies of World Missions*, ed. Terry, Smith and Anderson (Nashville: Broadman and Holman, 1998), 318.

9   Ibid.

10   Gordon C. Olson, *What in the World Is God Doing?* (Cedar Knolls, NJ: Global Gospel Publishers, 1994), 317.

11   Ibid., 317.

12   Gilliland, *The Word Among Us*, 2.

13   Sanchez, "Contextualization and the Missionary Endeavor," 318-327.

14   Hesselgrave and Rommen, *Contextualization: Meanings, Methods, and Models*, 31-35.

15   Charles Van Engen, *Mission on the Way: Issues in Mission Theology* (Grand Rapids: Baker Books, 1996), 72-73.

16   Ibid., 73.

17   Gilliland, *The Word Among Us*, viii.

[18] Charles Van Engen, Dean S. Gilliland and Paul Pierson, eds., *The Good News of the Kingdom: Mission Theology for the Third Millennium* (Maryknoll, NY: Orbis Books, 1993), 29.

[19] Ibid.

[20] Ibid., 29-30.

[21] Ibid., 30.

[22] Ibid., 30-31, 33.

[23] Paul G. Hiebert, *Anthropological Insights for Missionaries* (Grand Rapids: Baker Book House, 1985), 171, 184.

[24] Ibid., 184-185.

[25] Ibid., 186.

[26] Ibid., 186-192.

[27] Charles H. Kraft, *Christianity in Culture: A Study in Dynamic Biblical Theologizing in Cross-Cultural Perspective* (Maryknoll, NY: Orbis Books, 1979), 261-275.

[28] Sanchez, "Contextualization and the Missionary Endeavor," 330-333.

[29] Kraft, *Christianity in Culture*, 270-271, 267.

[30] Stan Guthrie, "Missiologists Take a Hard Look at Reasons for Gospel Resistance," *Occasional Bulletin of the Evangelical Missiological Society* 10, 1 (Winter 1998).

[31] Dudley J. Woodberry, ed., *Reaching the Resistant: Barriers and Bridges for Mission* (Pasadena, CA: William Carey Library, 1998), vii.

[32] Peter C. Wagner, *Strategies for Church Growth* (Ventura, CA: Regal Books, 1987), 78.

[33] Ibid., 81.

[34] Ibid.

[35] Charles Van Engen, "Reflecting Theologically about the Resistant," in *Reaching the Resistant: Barriers and Bridges for Mission* (Pasadena, CA: William Carey Library, 1998), 33.

[36] Ibid., 34.

[37] Ibid., 63.

[38] Peter C. Wagner, *Your Church Can Grow* (Ventura, CA: Regal Books, 1976), 57.

[39] Fred Hollander, *Leadership Dynamics: A Practical Guide to Effective Relationships* (New York: Free Press, 1978), 1.

[40] Lyle F. Schaller, *Getting Things Done* (Nashville: Abingdon, 1986), 86.

[41] Akio Morita, *Made in Japan* (New York: E.P. Dutton, 1986), 130-131.

[42] Robert C. Christopher, *The Japanese Mind* (London: Pan Books, 1984), 48.

[43] Gary Thomas, "The Return of the Jewish Church," *Christianity Today*, September 7, 1998, 63.

[44] Ibid.

[45] Ibid., 64.

[46] Ibid., 65.

[47] Phil Parshall, "Danger! New Directions in Contextualization," *Evangelical Missions Quarterly*, 34, 4 (October 1998): 404-410. For further research, see the explanation of the C1-C6 spectrum and two responses in the same issue, 407-417.

[48] John Travis, "The C1 to C6 Spectrum," *Evangelical Missions Quarterly*, 34, 4 (October 1998): 407-408.

[49] Parshall, "Danger! New Directions in Contextualization," 4, 405.

[50] Sanchez, "Contextualization and the Missionary Endeavor," 332-333.

The Role of Higher Education in the Christian World Mission: Past, Present and Future

Larry Poston

The Influence of Higher Education

Of the three institutions most closely associated with the Christian world mission—the local church, the theological school and the missionary sending agency—it is debatable as to which is the most *important*. Rather than becoming bogged down in what would most likely be a fruitless discussion regarding this question, I am going to pursue an altogether different line of inquiry. In the long run, it may be more productive to ask which of the three is the most *influential*, and in answer to this question, I would like to propose that the theological school is the linchpin of modern ministry-related endeavors.

With respect to the local church institution, for instance, the leadership—pastors, youth pastors and other administrative officials—almost without exception are the holders of, at least, a bachelor's degree. In the case of the pastorate, only in rare instances will a person without an M.Div. or its equivalent be employed in this day and age, and for churches which are large or which serve a higher socioeconomic class, a D.Min. or even a Ph.D. is becoming an expectation, if not a requirement. Thus all of the most influential persons within a local church structure have passed through at least one, and in most cases more than one, institution of higher learning.

With regard to mission agency personnel, it is difficult to imagine that the majority do not have a college degree—from the executive officers who lead the organization to the accountant who keeps track of the finances. Finally, it is the expectation of every credible missions organization that missionary candidates hold at least a bachelor's degree in some biblical or ministry-related field of study, and it is increasingly common to see men and women with masters and even doctoral degrees beginning the process of deputation. Higher education is thus the common denominator in each of these aspects of ministry involvement.

On the other hand, it is possible to become a missionary while bypassing a mission agency entirely. While the corps of "tentmakers" living abroad and engaged in missionary activity has never been large, awareness of this group has increased significantly over the last two decades. Some mission organizations have offered services to Christian businessmen, teachers, engineers and government workers abroad, providing loose structures of fellowship and accessibility to materials and counsel. But there is little direct influence, and even less overt control in all but a handful of cases.

Then there are the "lone ranger" missionaries, the independents who have heard a "call" and have made their way overseas in some fashion. Again, no direct connection with a mission agency is present. But nearly all of the members of both of these groups have been in schools of some kind—Bible institutes, Bible colleges, Christian liberal arts institutions, seminaries, universities—and even if these *alma maters* were not specifically "Christian," involvement in parachurch campus groups was often the spur which led to a missions emphasis while on an overseas assignment.

Parachurch experiences also make it possible to bypass the local church in one's spiritual development. Campus Crusade for Christ, InterVarsity Christian Fellowship, the Navigators and other similar groups have produced entire generations of Christians with tenuous connections to traditional local church structures. Many students make their way from university undergraduate programs to evangelical seminaries and thence to mission organizations. Short-term internships in local church situations may—or may not—be required in the course of seminary training. Some students merely continue their parachurch involvement when choosing a practical assignment. Candidates with interdenominational agencies, charged with raising their financial support from whatever sources they are able to discover, are sometimes fortunate enough to establish contacts with local churches seeking to extend their missionary outreach. Many candidates, however, rely almost totally on the support of individuals, and thus the influence of or involvement in the local church in their lives is minimized. And even those whose deputation experiences bring them in contact with church structures often have very little interpersonal contact other than the monthly financial contribution.

For these reasons we maintain that schools are the linchpins which hold the missionary enterprise together—or weaken it irreparably. It is the educational institutions, and those who teach in them, which bear the chief responsibility for the success or failure of the Christian world mission. The questions that we must therefore seek to answer are these: *Have educational institutions and their faculty members clearly understood their responsibility with regard to Christian missions? Are they taking the steps necessary to carry out this responsibility in an adequate fashion, given the current trends which exist both within higher education as well as within the missionary enterprise itself?*

Educating for Ministry—from Yesterday to Today

Currently, Christian institutions of higher learning are being forced to walk an incredibly narrow tightrope, bridging between academic integrity and credibility on the one hand and faithfulness to the Bible and the Great Commission on the other. Some schools have seemingly been more successful at walking this rope than others. It does not, for example, appear to have troubled most Roman Catholic institutions. Roman Catholic universities and colleges have maintained at least some semblance of religiosity while attaining enviable academic reputations. Notre Dame, Georgetown, Loyola, Fordham—the list is an impressive one.

But Protestants have not been successful at developing institutions that have stayed the course. The Ivy League universities—nearly all of which were founded and sponsored by Protestant denominations—have been sundered from their religious roots and rate only the term "secular" at the present time. And the Bible institutes, Bible colleges, Christian liberal arts colleges and seminaries established by conservative evangelicals have never attained either the academic or societal status that Catholic universities have acquired.[1]

The absence of such status was not a problem in the past. Indeed, one can easily substantiate the claim that a primary reason for the failure of these Christian institutions to attain the heights of academic respectability was simply that they never aspired to do so. Their very establishment was an act of protest against much of what the drive for academic "respectability" had produced; namely, institutions which not only sidelined all attempts to discover aspects of spirituality and the divine, but which in many cases openly ridiculed such aspects in the context of academic pursuits. For most evangelicals, acceptance and approval of their own institutions from "Ivy League" schools would have been a mark of failure in that such acceptance would have signaled nothing less than an apostate status.[2]

Therefore, A.B. Simpson's Missionary Training Institute, Jonathan Blanchard's Wheaton College (begun as the Illinois Bible Institute), Lewis Sperry Chafer's Dallas Theological Seminary and other such schools forged new paths of their own. And for the majority of these schools, such concepts as "state approval" and "regional accreditation" were of no concern for the first several decades of their existence. Students in these institutions were, for the most part, adequately equipped to perform the tasks of evangelism, disciplemaking, Christian education and church planting. Pastors, missionaries and Christian educators were the products of these institutions, and they carried out the Great Commission in accordance with a Pietistic interpretation of the Bible's texts, emphasizing the internal and personal transformation of the individual rather than an external and institutional development of society.

This Pietistic emphasis contributed in part to the nearly unanimous adoption of dispensational premillennialism by evangelicals in the opening years of the twentieth century and the concomitant rejection of the amillennial and postmillennial eschatologies of historic Protestantism. Consequently, the focus of the Christian world mission shifted from national and global concerns—such as extending the kingdom of God in a physical sense through expansion of the institutional Church—to a strictly individualist orientation. Dispensational premillennialists had no intention of establishing a worldwide Christian culture—which would have involved a much more holistic approach to the education of converts—but was instead primarily concerned with "bringing back the King"—an event which could be hastened by concentrating solely upon the task of "preaching the Gospel to every creature."[3]

The establishment of "Christian" political, economic, judicial and other such structures—tasks which would require a basic liberal arts education in addition to Bible training—was considered a colossal waste of time, given the presumption that due to the innate sinfulness of all human beings—including the Christian populace—the King would be forced upon His return to dismantle any and all earthly structures (including those established by Christians) in order to build His millennial kingdom.

Paradigm Shifts in Evangelical Higher Education

Three major changes occurred after World War II which had the effect of producing a new focus on the part of Christian institutions of higher learning. First, *evangelicalism began to undergo a subtle transformation with regard to its "Christ and Culture" philosophy.* Using H. Richard Niebuhr's paradigm, one can maintain that prior to the war, dispensational premillennialism had placed its adherents either in the "Christ Against Culture" category or the "Christ and Culture in Paradox" position.[4] Both of these perspectives marginalized evangelicals not only from the standpoint of secular society, but also from the perspective of a large portion of "Christianity" (i.e., the mainline Protestant denominations) as well.

As we observed earlier, such marginalization was not problematic for Christians living in the late 1800s and early 1900s. But the devastation to human civilization wrought by World War II in the 1940s, the crass materialism and rise of communism in the 1950s, and the political, social and moral liberalization of the 1960s forced evangelicals to ask themselves if they had been correct to concentrate so exclusively upon the individual aspects of human life; perhaps something needed to be said about external and institutional concerns after all.

But it was immediately apparent that the transformation of *cultural institutions* requires a much different form of education than that which existed in conservative Christian colleges. New curricula involving the humanities and the social sciences had to be developed, and the only extant models for such curricula were in the secular colleges and universities. In order to provide this education from a Christian perspective, it was necessary either to draw upon Christians who had earned their degrees from secular institutions or to send teachers who had gained their credentials exclusively through Christian institutions to acquire further education within the secular university system.

When a person receives his or her undergraduate education from a Bible institute or Bible college, proceeds to a seminary graduate program, gains experience through involvement in a pastorate or missionary context for several years and then returns to a teaching position in a Christian institution, a cycle is formed which permits only a minimum of new ideas to enter a curricular program. But when men and women are drawn in from "the outside" (i.e., a secular educational environment) or when Christians are sent to be educated within such an environment, the concepts which then enter the pool of Christian ideas contain drastically different philosophical (not to mention theological) underpinnings.

The effect of such ideas upon Bible college and seminary curricula has been profound, and the consequent effect upon those educated in accordance with such curricula—including missionary candidates and aspiring pastors—has been profound as well. We will return to this theme shortly.

A second post-war change concerns *the kind and quality of the education provided by Christian institutions of higher learning*. The expectations of evangelical Christians regarding what their educational systems should be characterized by have been shaped in recent years by various media which have published comparative data regarding institutions of higher learning in the United States. The availability of such rankings to the Christian public has led many to question why evangelical institutions—with only a handful of exceptions—never appear in such rankings. The implication, of course, is that the education received at such institutions is of such poor quality that they have been completely excluded from the charts.

Not long ago, such neglect by secular rating systems would have been worn as a badge of honor. In addition, the fact that the secular rating systems use somewhat subjective criteria for their assignments should be of significance.[5] But separatist "badges of honor" are no longer worn by evangelicals, and *perception*—rather than objective data—has become the order of the day. As a result, parents who are doling out increasingly higher tuition fees for their sons and daughters to attend Christian institutions of higher learning have begun to conclude that they are not getting sufficient value for their dollars.

Consequently, Christian institutions have been faced with two options, neither of which is attractive. They can adapt their curricular programs and campus environments to compete with the institutions that are ranked at or near the top of the rating systems—these institutions being essentially secular in orientation—or they can look forward to a slow decline in their student populations and eventually close their doors.

The desire of parents to receive more value for their college expenditures is not the only financial pressure brought to bear on Christian institutions, leading to yet a third change in the educational enterprise. *Rising costs have forced an increasing number of schools to seek state and regional accreditation in order to become eligible to receive and award federal and state grants and loans*. Lacking the resources to supply financial aid in significant amounts to students, Christian institutions have been unable to compete with state and private universities which receive heavy subsidies from both government and private agencies.

To meet accreditation requirements, certain compromises have been necessary in the areas of curriculum and institutional ethos. George Marsden, for instance, cites the example of New York State, which has "withheld aid from religiously affiliated colleges until they furnished satisfactory evidence that religious considerations were secondary to defining the tasks of the college. . . . [S]uch pressures as well as those growing out of parallel court decisions of the era sped the processes of secularization for many colleges."[6]

Since, as we have established previously, nearly all of the current generation of pastors, youth leaders, missionary candidates and missionary agency personnel have passed through these institutions, we must conclude that the changes noted above have affected the Christian world mission in a number of ways.

With regard to the various Christian educational institutions, it is perhaps the situation of the Christian liberal arts colleges which should be of greatest concern at the present. Bible institutes, Bible colleges and seminaries do not stand in nearly as dangerous a position. Why is this the case?

Most Bible colleges have acquired state and, in some cases, even regional accreditation and are able to offer baccalaureate degrees in a very limited number of fields (i.e., Bible and music). In order to meet accreditation standards, these schools have added a minimal number of liberal arts courses, all of which are taught from an undeniably Christian perspective, most often by professors who have obtained either a "mixed" education (i.e., both "secular" and "sacred") or an exclusively "Christian" one. These liberal arts courses have enhanced the typical Bible college curriculum by injecting elements of the social sciences and humanities which have broadened the horizons of the students in attendance.

Bible and theology courses, however, continue to be the mainstay of the overall course of study, in most cases comprising one-third to one-half of the total number of required credits. Thus a Bible college graduate comes away with an extensive knowledge of the Bible and theology; this knowledge will be expanded and sharpened by the seminary experience which nearly all who today plan to enter full-time Christian service eventually obtain. Thus the traditional criticisms of Bible institute and Bible college education (i.e., no accreditation and no broad-based general education requirements) have to a large extent been addressed.

The Christian liberal arts college, however, seeks accreditation for a large number of majors, including subjects in the humanities, social sciences, natural sciences and technological fields. The push to enhance the liberal arts aspects of these schools has in many cases eroded the Bible and theology content of general education requirements to an absolute minimum, such as one or two courses.

An evaluation of evangelical seminaries yields much the same conclusion as was drawn regarding Bible colleges and institutes. The purpose of such graduate institutions is to prepare men and women for professional ministerial functions, and therefore most of the curricula offered in these schools are heavily weighted in favor of Bible and theology courses. This is not always the case, however, and so it would be useful to distinguish between the various categories of entering students and the types of programs available to them at the graduate level, for different combinations of these categories will yield varying products. At least four combinations can be suggested:

Category #1: *The graduate of a Bible college or institute who prepares for ministry through attainment of a master of divinity seminary degree.* Such a combination essentially adds an additional three or four years of biblical and theological studies to the four years of introductory level courses acquired at the undergraduate level.

Category #2: *The graduate of a Bible college or institute who prepares for ministry through a master of arts seminary degree.* If this graduate level degree is in Old Testament, New Testament or systematic theology, further education in biblical studies is, of course, forthcoming. A master's degree in missions or Christian education, however, moves the student into a very different set of academic disciplines. For the aspiring missionary, studies in anthropology, linguistics, comparative religions and urban ministry will most likely be the standard bill of fare. Built upon a Bible college or institute background, these studies have the effect of broadening one's education in directions helpful to one's professional aspirations, although further training in purely biblical studies will most likely be minimal.

Category #3: *The graduate of a liberal arts college or university who prepares for ministry through attainment of a master of divinity seminary degree.* In most such cases, the undergraduate degree will be in a field unrelated to Bible or theology. Thus the seminary program must bear the full responsibility for preparing such a student both in terms of biblical/theological knowledge *and* in terms of professional ministerial training. Since statistically speaking this is the most common type of student found in evangelical seminaries, most such institutions have adapted their programs to meet these needs. At the completion of his or her formal training, however, the student in category 3 will most likely have up to sixty or so credits *less* of Bible and theology instruction than his or her colleague who is in category 1.

Category #4: *The graduate of a liberal arts college or university who prepares for ministry through attainment of a master of arts seminary degree.* Again, if this degree is in the area of Old Testament, New Testament or systematic theology, at least some training in biblical studies is acquired, though not nearly to the extent of one enrolled in a master of divinity program, and certainly not to an extent even distantly comparable to the category 1 student.

The student in this category who chooses to major in missions (or some other than purely biblical field) will without a doubt be the "weakest" in terms of overall Bible preparation. As noted above, the courses in this program of study will revolve around anthropology, communications, urban studies and the like. *Some* Bible courses will, of course, be required, but this will be a minimal amount. The question that all mission agencies must ask is whether or not the candidate who is a category 4 graduate is adequately prepared to be a minister of the gospel in cross-cultural situations. It may indeed be the case that category 1 students are, by comparison, "overqualified," but would it not be so that those in category 4 might be dangerously *underqualified* to fulfill the aspect of the Great Commission that requires ministers of the gospel to teach new disciples to obey everything that Jesus commanded (Matthew 28:20)?

Some might object that if the category 4 person was a graduate of a *Christian* liberal arts college, the "danger" suggested here might be mitigated. But to be frank, this may not be the case at all. It is even conceivable that a student who has graduated from a fully secular institution might actually be better off with regard to Bible and theology training than one who has attended a Christian liberal arts college. Let me explain.

The Christian liberal arts college is not a new concept; indeed, many of the earliest Protestant institutions of higher learning such as Harvard, Yale, Princeton, Brown and Northwestern could be said to have been Christian liberal arts institutions at the time of their inception. The title is now reserved, however, for schools which have banded together around a specific set of criteria, in the main espousing a conservative view of the Bible as the inspired Word of God and a likewise conservative approach to the interpretation and application of the Scriptures within the context of life and society.

James Davison Hunter, professor of sociology at the University of Virginia, has been a leading researcher into trends involving evangelicals, including evangelical higher education. His study of nine leading evangelical liberal arts colleges and seven seminaries, published in 1987, noted several disturbing trends in these schools. Stated simply, the educational process of these institutions often serves to *undermine* the religious commitment of students rather than strengthening it. With statistical support, Hunter claims that "the more intent evangelical higher education is on preserving the integrity of its traditions, the less successful it is. . . . Among Protestant colleges, the more serious a commitment to the task of higher education, the more prevalent the liberalization and secularization tendencies."[7]

This last statement could well be interpreted in the following manner: the better the institution is from the standpoint of secular ranking systems—the standards which "count" with contemporary parents and students—the more likely the institution is to "secularize" its students. It would thus be tempting to conclude that the *lower* an evangelical institution is ranked by such systems, the better an institution it will be from the standpoint of biblical values. A college or seminary which does not appear at all on these lists could presumably wear this omission as a badge of biblical integrity. But such conclusions—even if they are warranted—are essentially without value at the current juncture of history.

This is so for two reasons. First, it would be impossible to convince the parents of college-age young people of the truth of such logic, for the plausibility structure of our time disallows the separatist notions that accompanied the establishment of the early Bible institutes. The argument that approval by a secularist ranking system is indicative of spiritual decline might conceivably have succeeded in the last quarter of the nineteenth century, but not during the corresponding period in the twentieth. Secondly, it would be even more difficult to convince the faculties and administrative personnel of the evangelical institutions which are now beginning to appear on the lists of "quality" institutions that all of the striving they have undergone to attain academic respectability has actually resulted in a decline in their spirituality. Suggesting that they should seek a *lower* position in ranking systems would be considered ludicrous in the extreme.

Given our current cultural context, we must seek to attack these problems in another manner, one which adopts the somewhat optimistic presupposition that biblical integrity and academic respectability need not necessarily be inversely proportional. But I shall leave this topic for the final section of the essay. Presently it is necessary to enter into a discussion of yet another topic so that when we begin to assemble our conclusions, we will have all the necessary components at our disposal.

Current Trends in Education and Their Implications for the Christian World Mission

If, as we have claimed, institutions of higher learning are the clearinghouses for church leadership, mission agency leadership and missionary personnel, then we can expect that trends in education will eventually make their presence known within both church and mission contexts. It is thus incumbent upon Christian denominations and mission agencies to keep their fingers on the pulses of the schools from which their most significant personnel are drawn. It is also incumbent upon these schools to assume responsibility for the physical, intellectual and spiritual development of the men and women who enter their halls and engage in the pursuit of truth. Part of this responsibility involves an awareness of the constantly changing profile of today's students. The following are some of the more significant trends that currently exist.

1. *Older Students.* Demographically, the pool of students in the traditional college age range of eighteen to twenty-two years has declined significantly during the last three decades. This may be difficult to observe at first, since a much larger *proportion* of persons in this age range attend college now than was true in previous generations. Many begin college programs—and so the numbers look good. But a large percentage of these persons are not adequately gifted or prepared to withstand the rigors of a college education, and so less than half of those who begin actually complete a four-year degree.[8] Thus the generation of eighteen to twenty-two-year-olds can no longer be expected to supply the recruiting needs of tuition-driven institutions, and therefore other markets are being tapped.

A result of this change in demographics is the growing popularity of degree completion programs, designed specifically for persons who began a college career but who for one reason or another never completed their program. These persons reenter the academic environment at a (usually) much older age, and a number of these persons plan to use their degree to facilitate a career change. Sometimes the change is to a ministry-related field; the person has experienced the new birth, developed a desire to be involved in pastoral or missionary ministry, learned that a certain amount of education is required and, because of a "late start" attitude, seeks to complete this academic training in as rapid a manner as possible.

Most undergraduate degree completion programs require one or two years. Seminary or graduate school training—almost universally required for the pastorate and increasingly necessary for missionary service—adds another two to four years. Acquisition of the requisite educational credentials can thus take from three to six years. For persons who begin in their late twenties, thirties or forties, time spent in the classroom can easily boost the age at which they assume full-time ministerial responsibilities into the next decade of their life. And candidates with faith mission agencies can look forward to a two- or three-year support-raising period in addition to their completion of educational requirements.

2. *Dysfunctional Family Backgrounds.* As the rates of divorce and remarriage continue to hover at approximately fifty percent of all marital relationships, the familial experiences of students entering Christian institutions of higher learning are, in perhaps a majority of cases, very different from the situations of previous generations. Effects include either a profound distrust of and skepticism regarding the institution of marriage in general, or an overly eager desire to find a marriage partner and "succeed" where one's parents failed.

The first attitude produces a delay in entering into serious relationships until the late twenties or even beyond, which from the standpoint of personal spiritual formation may be good (in that more time is devoted to undistracted physical, intellectual and spiritual development) or bad (when the temptations of the profoundly immoral modern world beset the single Christian). The second attitude may produce a motivation strong enough to make a marriage succeed at any cost, or it may result in ideals and expectations which are so unreasonable that the union is destined to fail before it even begins, thus renewing the cycle of divorce and remarriage.

Students arrive at institutions of higher education with a host of family-oriented problems which can manifest themselves in ministerial situations long after the educational process is completed, and it is clear that the stresses of cross-cultural adjustment can exacerbate these problems to the point where new missionary candidates will break down under the strain. Mission agencies and churches which insist upon appointing or employing only "well-adjusted" individuals without such backgrounds are most likely already feeling the strain of a vastly decreased pool of qualified candidates. To fill the constant—and in many cases increasing—number of available positions, denominations and independent missions agencies are often forced to choose persons who are a "risk," necessitating the establishment of counseling programs for those who, under normal circumstances, would be expected to be spiritual counselors themselves.

3. *"Attention Deficit Syndrome."* By this characteristic I do not mean the hyperactivity of elementary school children whose attention span has been synchronized to television programming, but rather the observed inability of contemporary young people to fix their minds and wills upon a single task until completion. Educators recognize this syndrome as a generic "sign of the times" which spans the entire spectrum of student cohorts and carries over into one's work and career.

The trend manifests itself at the college level in the number of changes that students make in their choice of academic majors within a single school or transfers between two or more schools. It appears in an employment history in the multiple career changes that have become the subject of a variety of studies. This unsettledness is in large part a legacy of our national commitment to pluralistic democracy and the individual liberation brought about by modern industrialization and the technology of rapid transportation. Automatic inheritance of the occupation of one's parent and residence in close proximity to one's relatives are now so rare as to be anomalous at this juncture of history. The "global village" beckons and the adventurousness glamorized by the media "Indiana Joneses" both mirrors and influences contemporary social trends.

Affordable semester-abroad programs and summer missions trips have also contributed to the mobile orientation of young people—and the consequences for schools, churches and mission agencies are profound. The phenomenon manifests itself most noticeably in brief tenures at local churches and in "short-term" missionary stints. Concerning the latter, rhetoric is now regularly heard from the standpoint of the champions of "life-long" and "career missionary" service which is either subtly or blatantly patronizing of young people who cannot "stay the course." The implication is that the "older" missionaries were (or are) "tougher" and "more enduring," but such attitudes are misguided and will eventually prove to be counterproductive.

Like it or not, "short-term" missions are the future of the missionary enterprise and, as some of the more innovative missions thinkers are beginning to write, such strategies can be seen as a return to the pattern established by Paul, who, when all is said and done, spent no longer than three years in any one place and, according to the reckoning of certain commentators, dedicated no more than a total of nine years to cross-cultural ministry.[9] While it is true that Paul did not have to spend time in language acquisition—an important distinction between his experience and that of present-day missionary personnel—there is still room for a great deal of innovative thinking with regard to efficient and effective short-term missionary involvement.

4. *Undisciplined Lifestyles.* In the recent past, the peoples of North America and Northern Europe were characterized by a work ethic and view of the concept of "progress" that were in many ways unique in the history of humanity. To a great degree, these characteristics were a legacy of the influence of Christianity in a generic sense.[10] Other contributions of this generalized religious sociology were a linear view of history and a sense of "mission" which impelled Westerners to the "cutting edge" of scientific and technological achievement, resulting in improved health and hygiene, lengthened life spans and increased leisure time for pursuits other than physical survival. The "double filtration" undergone by American immigrants produced highly motivated, disciplined and entrepreneurial men and women.[11] The rigor of the requirements of general college curricula in bygone years testifies to the kinds of students that were produced by the set of conditions described above.[12]

Since the 1950s, however, there has been a change in the profile of the "typical American." Contemporary studies speak of a "culture of narcissism" and "a culture of disbelief"[13] having replaced traditional American values. The increase in leisure time coupled with the development of work- and time-saving technological advancements have led to a "flabbiness" in the American psyche which was not present in previous generations. Gone is the "ruggedness" that accompanied the pioneer spirit of early Americans; instead we find an addiction to modern amenities which weaken the body and stifle the mind. The "Protestant work ethic" has given way to a demand for extended vacations and "flex-time," and the former preoccupation with "the great outdoors" and sportsmanship has evolved into a lounge-chair-by-the-pool lifestyle with a portable television tuned to a baseball game.

This lack of discipline has carried over as well into the realm of morality and ethics. Increases in sexual promiscuity, marital infidelity, divorce and open homosexuality have been paralleled by demands for abortion rights, the legalization of marijuana, voluntary euthanasia and the protection of pornography under the First Amendment. The ready availability of the latter via cable television, video and the Internet has produced an unparalleled access to visual experiences which in the past were reserved only for the most depraved elements of society.

All of the above have combined to change the general profile of today's college students—Christian as well as non-Christian—into something quite different from previous generations. As mentioned earlier, the young men and women who walk the halls of our Bible institutes, Christian liberal arts colleges and seminaries are as likely as not to be the products of broken marriages and as such have been exposed to an environment in which little or no discipline has been exercised with regard to interpersonal relationships inside—or outside—of marriage. These students have viewed thousands of hours of television and motion pictures, the overwhelming majority of which have glorified immoral, gluttonous and materialistic lifestyles which are a mockery of the entire concept of a disciplined life. Study skills are undeveloped or nonexistent; reading and writing competencies verge in many cases on functional illiteracy. And the real tragedy, of course, is that the persons who have met the requirements for matriculation in institutions of higher learning are among the "brightest and best" that America is currently producing.

Most of the students who remain in a program eventually acquire enough of the skills and discipline necessary for completion of a college degree. But some of those who receive their diplomas and present themselves as candidates for employment to mission agencies and church denominations have shed very little of the psychological and emotional baggage they brought with them from their home life. The camaraderie and supportive environment of dormitory life, along with a busy academic schedule, can serve to submerge some of the wounds for a time, but many of these may well reappear once this season of life is past. And to have such scars reopened in the midst of cross-cultural—or congregational—adjustment can be a horrific ordeal indeed.

5. *Shallow worldviews.* Ours is an age of "nowness"; there is little—if any—sense of the past. Radio and television commentaries speak in

terms of "the worst storm since 1987" or "the best cost of living index since 1992" as though these statements have actual historical significance, and "tradition" is a concept that is openly denigrated by persons from both secular and "Christian" society. For Christians, such a lack of perspective isolates each individual in a niche so tiny and insignificant that any sense of "mission" is lost completely. Communicating to students that they are participants in a divine "search and rescue operation" which has been ongoing since the dawn of earth's existence may evoke nothing more than a vacant stare. Somehow the idea doesn't sound nearly as exciting as becoming a "Raider of the Lost Ark."

One might be tempted to see the beginnings of a correction to this state of affairs in the recent return of some conservative Protestant Christians to denominations and rites which are much more deeply rooted in history than the newer "low-church movements." In keeping with this trend, evangelicals are showing a renewed interest in both the Roman Catholic and Eastern Orthodox churches.[14] But there are serious questions as to whether this trend should be viewed as a true reformation (or counter-reformation, as the case may be), for the majority of participants are able to explore such alternatives only at the expense of biblically based theological reflection. In many—perhaps most—cases, it is the exoticness of the experience which is attractive rather than a true sense of tradition, and thus shallowness is still present, albeit in a new form.

For those who have not found the above-mentioned trend attractive, the lack of "rootedness" which accompanies a shallow worldview manifests itself in several ways. In the schools, it appears in the readiness of students to change majors and/or institutions with no thought given to the historical background of the institutions that are chosen. Issues of geographic location and financial aid have replaced such items as denominational or theological loyalty. A shallow worldview ultimately results in an insecure—or nonexistent—base of operations, and therefore one lacks the "sense of self" so necessary to be able to adapt to a congregation or a culture.[15]

6. *Global naiveté.* With the advent of satellite relay systems, the human race has never been so aware of its various ethnic and cultural components as it is today. Comparatively inexpensive air travel has made overseas summer "missions" trips possible for church youth groups, college students and other lay persons in general.

As with many of the trends we have noted, this phenomenon is two-edged. Such short-term exposure to foreign missions contexts can be—and in many cases has been—extremely positive. Mission agencies in particular note that a significant percentage of young people who participate in summer missions programs return later as career missionaries. Another positive aspect is that some young people discover that cross-cultural adjustment is not a part of their personal giftedness and they consequently eliminate direct missionary involvement from their future plans. Such a filtration process can save a great deal of anguish and embarrassment at a later time.

The downside, however, is that some young people gain an unrealistic perspective on the nature of missionary activity. The period of time spent in a foreign context is either too short or too sheltered—or both—to allow the participants to experience the vicissitudes of "culture shock." They return with a sense of "That was easy!" or "That was fun!" whereas long-term evangelism, disciplemaking and church planting are far from easy and are rarely characterized by those who are most closely involved as "fun."

For others, the experience is one of adventure—the thrill of visiting exotic locations with opportunities for photography and the acquisition of artifacts with which one's bedroom or dormitory room can be decorated. For this group, the spiritual or theological elements regarding the communication of the gospel in order to elicit decisions for Christ and thus procure eternal life for lost men and women are often given strictly secondary or even tertiary priority. The "adventure" is the thing. And yet a third group may take the attitude that their international ministry involvement is now accomplished. They have functioned as "missionaries" and in so doing have "conquered" that bit of life and are now ready to move on to whatever is next on the list of "things to experience."

The above observations are by no means intended to disparage the continuation of summer or other short-term programs. However, mission agencies and churches should be cautious regarding the format of such ventures; unless they are carefully planned and staffed by the proper personnel and include time for special debriefing at their conclusion, they could conceivably produce the exact opposite of what they are intended for.

A Vision for the Future

There are other trends that could be discussed,[16] but the ones above are the most significant. In a sense, students with the above characteristics represent the "raw material" that enters our Christian institutions of higher learning. It is entirely conceivable that in many cases, this "material" exits these schools molded into new forms but with all of the above-mentioned "impurities" still present in the final product. And such impurities are in actuality structural weaknesses which under stressful conditions can fail at critical junctures. Thus it becomes the responsibility of our educational institutions to do much more than merely produce *educated* older students from broken families with short-term mentalities who are undisciplined, shallow and naive with regard to international issues. The "raw material" must be reshaped and these impurities either removed or reduced to insignificant proportions. How might such an effect be produced?

The very first adaptation which today's institutions of higher learning must undergo is to *come to terms with the "raw material" we as educators are being given to work with*. Many faculty members bemoan that the time is seemingly gone forever when entering freshmen had a modicum of preparation: they could read, write, pay attention, take notes, fulfill the requisite assignments and enter into stable career tracks. But there is little to be gained by yearning for "the good old days."[17] Educators must rise to the challenge of a generation of students with new characteristics calling for revisions in traditional educational programs. The following are some suggestions regarding a new paradigm for Christian higher education.

1. *Welcome and utilize the special qualities of older students.* Their experience and (hopefully) their maturity should be celebrated. Presumably their motivation level is high, particularly those who are in the midst of career changes. For the schools, the following innovations are suggested. As much as possible, the work and/or ministry experiences of older students should be incorporated into classroom discussions and seminar formats. There should be opportunities for individuals to share brief oral presentations that can serve as practical illustrations from life and starting points for "street level" discussions. Course assignments should be designed so that several "options" are presented with regard to projects, essay topics and the like so that the needs of both younger, inexperienced students as well as older, more seasoned veterans will be met.

Older *married* students should be tracked into a degree completion program with all possible haste and from there into a seminary or graduate school. My reasons for this suggestion are multiple. First, at nearly every undergraduate institution, the relatively small cadre of married students is an anomaly which few schools have been able to fit into their overall environment. In most cases, such persons live off campus, are employed off campus at (usually) odd hours and often celebrate their independence as nonresidential students. Their ties with professors outside of the classroom are tenuous at best. The creation of programs to "fold them into" the school at large are in all but exceptional cases doomed to failure. But a well-structured degree completion program builds these students into cohorts which function as support groups in ways that traditional undergraduate programs never do for married students. Secondly, these curricula are usually *accelerated* programs which also award credit for "life experiences." These two factors save the student both time and money—important considerations when one is older and has a family. Thirdly, these programs generally meet only one night per week, leaving opportunity for employment and the attendance of family responsibilities. For all but a few married students, these characteristics are ideal.

Arguments against older missionary candidates have traditionally included issues of language acquisition and family concerns. These aspects can be addressed by our Christian schools—both undergraduate and graduate—if they are willing to step out of traditional molds. I will deal with the issue of family in the following section. With regard to language study, infinitely higher standards for foreign languages must be introduced in schools which provide training for ministry among peoples of other cultures and languages.

This upgrading should begin at the undergraduate level and make use of techniques more focused on oral ability than has traditionally been the case. Educational institutions—both undergraduate and graduate—which have required New Testament Greek as part of their Bible or ministry curriculum should seriously consider allowing more flexibility for students intending overseas or inner city ministries.[18] Studies in Spanish, Portuguese, French, Swahili, Arabic, Russian, Chinese and Japanese should be supported and staffed either as courses taught by adjuncts or as supervised audiovisual programs. Every effort should be made to utilize—or create—language programs which produce students who are fluent communicators in major foreign languages while still in the United States.

For their part, mission agencies must begin to re-think their age limitations. Cutoff points such as the early thirties will need to be moved upward or made more flexible. Historically, it is relatively easy to demonstrate that nearly all of the earliest missionaries to foreign lands (i.e., Patrick, Columba, Columban, Boniface, etc.) were in their forties or beyond when they began their ministries—and this in a day when the average life expectancy was considerably shorter. With life expectancies currently reaching into the eighties, and with projections of the nineties and hundreds in the near future, there is no reason why "older" missionaries cannot be expected to have ministries equally as fruitful as younger candidates.[19]

2. *Give serious consideration to the ideas of celibacy or limited family size.* I am aware of how "touchy" such topics can be, especially in an age of evangelical "focus on the family." While family values have been a popular issue since the 1970s, and marriage and child-rearing remain "sacred" and "inviolable" traditions among contemporary conservative Christians, I believe that we as evangelicals must seriously consider developing a corps of men and women who have discerned in themselves a gift of celibacy. There are several reasons for my advocacy of such a position.

First and foremost, the apostle Paul—often held to be the "prototypical missionary"—recommends the non-married state, particularly in conjunction with "crisis" situations (1 Corinthians 7:26). While such a description would perhaps not be appropriate for a large part of today's world, the fact that between two-thirds and three-quarters of the global population is currently unreachable by "traditional" missionaries presents us with a situation calling for what may be considered "extreme" measures. Single missionaries are both physically and psychologically less encumbered than married missionaries, and are consequently freer to risk clandestine entry into "closed" countries for involvement in cutting-edge evangelism, disciplemaking and church planting. As an earlier mission agency motto put it: "There are no 'closed' countries—as long as you're not worried about coming back." Only singles truly have this kind of freedom.

Secondly, this recommendation deals in a nontraditional way with the characteristic of "broken families." What we often fail to admit to ourselves is that for many of our young men and women, the emotional and even physical scarring of a shattered family background has made the "ideal" of the "biblical family model" which is presented by churches and Christian schools either undesirable or unattainable.

It is highly unfortunate that the alternative of celibacy is often derided by these same institutions as "anomalous" or "medieval," whereas biblically speaking it is neither of these. Voluntary celibacy may actually become a haven of healing and a source for dynamic Christian ministry.[20] Undistracted devotion to the Lord and undivided commitment to a life of ministry could very well become a welcome option to many of today's students. Faculty members, counselors, pastors and mission agencies alike should embrace and even in certain circumstances recommend this institution.

Among evangelicals, children are held to be a "heritage of the LORD." Even the suggestion that one might choose to have no children or limit one's family size to one or two children for the sake of ministry draws fire from a number of evangelicals.[21] Many missionaries are at pains to show that their offspring greatly enhance their ability to identify with the adherents of specific cultures. While this may be true in some cases, it is also undeniable that the testimony of the historical record does not bear out the claim that couples with children are more effective or productive in their ministries.

Again, from the standpoint of freedom and flexibility, single missionaries or childless couples are able to devote infinitely more time and energy to ministry endeavors. A childless couple is able to function as an undivided team; the wife does not feel separated from the ministry, does not miss out on language study and is not closed off from the culture as sometimes happens in the midst of child-rearing. The problems associated with schooling—either those involving the separation of parents and children through boarding schools or those involved in the placement of children within foreign public or private schools—are eliminated entirely, as is the risk of the psychological malformation observed in many of these situations.

One of the darker secrets of the modern missionary movement (as well as the pastorate) is the number of broken families and damaged children that have resulted from the inability of a large number of ministers to maintain a proper balance between family and ministry.[22] Thus the options of celibacy or limited family size should be made available to today's ministry aspirants, and it is within the context of our educational institutions—through chapel sessions, courses on contemporary issues and carefully chosen conference speakers—that such seeds can be sown.

3. *Develop short-term, "strike force" mentalities and the concept of "seasonal" approaches to career missions.* Rather than continuing to castigate today's young people for their lack of long-term commitment, we must capitalize on their shorter bursts of energy. Such adaptation may take two forms. The first would be an expansion and refinement of the already existing and explosively expanding phenomenon of short-term missions.[23]

The Christian and Missionary Alliance has, for instance, developed the concept of a "mobile strike force;" missionaries who are already residing and ministering in various countries around the world but who are "on call" and ready to move to any location which through an apparent work of God has become receptive and productive. Another example is the CoMission cooperative effort. When it became apparent that the former Soviet Union was undergoing a state of dissolution and that a window of opportunity was opening for Christian missionary activity, a number of mission agencies pulled seasoned veterans from fields where work was well-developed and moved them to Russia.

A second approach would involve a more deliberate utilization of the current pattern of alternating periods of overseas ministry and "home service." Each overseas term and home assignment could be cast as completely independent segments of missionaries' lives. Each of these time periods would thus become in effect a "short-term" assignment, with clear goals and objectives partitioned off by a starting date and an ending date. Some missionaries might need to be moved around within a single country or even within a specific geographic area in order to curb the restlessness that appears to infect a large number of today's young people. If not the geographic location, then perhaps the specific ministry or work assignment could be changed on a regular basis.

For a number of "baby boomers" and "busters," a variety of experiences is considered necessary to develop one's "self" or "full potential." This is not necessarily a "New Age" concept as some have categorized it, for the Bible indicates that we are all "being transformed into his likeness with ever-increasing glory" (2 Corinthians 3:18), implying a process of development toward maturity. Providing such a means of self-fulfillment for missionaries and pastors could become an integral part of both mission and denominational planning processes.

Here, of course, our educational institutions will need to partner with mission agencies and local churches to introduce and cultivate the concept of a series of "short-term" or "seasonal" involvement while playing on the same "team" for life. "Team loyalty" is certainly understood within the context of athletics. The same mind-set must be created in today's students with regard to a mission organization or denomination. We must encourage our young people to choose a team—carefully and with much consideration—and then stick with that team for life.

4. *Cultivate an "elitist" mentality.* Perhaps the greatest service our Christian schools can render to individuals is the inculcation of an "elitist" mentality in them. It is unfortunate that the historically recent

trend has been to reduce Christians to a level of "humility" that is more culturally defined than biblically prescribed. In actuality, the Bible abounds with images of the people of God as an elite group. The children of Israel were a "holy, called-out and elect people"—the "apple of God's eye." The New Testament saints are "the Bride of Christ" and *"a chosen people, a royal priesthood, a holy nation, a people belonging to God"* (1 Peter 2:9, emphasis added).

Christians are the sons and daughters of God, princes and princesses in the kingdom of heaven, citizens and ambassadors of that kingdom, living on earth to fulfill a special commission at the completion of which they will obtain specially prepared dwelling places in a city built for them by God Himself. The New Testament writers consistently call all readers to ponder and apply such concepts of identity; Paul urges each of the Galatians, for instance, to *"test his own actions. Then he can take pride in himself, without comparing himself to somebody else"* (Galatians 6:4, emphasis added). In the fullness of confidence born of our understanding of who we are in Christ, we are to acknowledge our highborn position and giftedness and from that secure base serve mankind in a number of ways.

Throughout history, an appeal to elitism has shown its worth time and time again. The sense of "self" and of "mission" coupled with the discipline required both to attain and maintain elite status has set the adherents of elite groups in a far different class from that of the masses. While the context has usually been military—the Green Berets, the Army Rangers, the Navy SEALs—occasionally the phenomenon has appeared in the history of the Church. The Society of Jesus, for instance, was able to capitalize on the *mystique* of elitism, producing in the process one of the most highly educated and skillful groups of people in history.[24]

But we as evangelicals appear to be so afraid of arousing "pride" in our young people that we reduce our educational curricula to a set of "general requirements" which are applied to all alike, despite the indisputable fact that the giftedness of students differs tremendously from one individual to the next. While there is little hope of doing away with general education curricula, measures can be instituted which will address the situation "at the other end," so to speak. Through "honors" courses—classes which require a minimum grade point average, for instance—crafting can take place in ways which are not practicable in most general classes.

Some will object that intellectual giftedness should not be the only criteria for an "elite" designation, particularly as applied within Christian contexts. This is entirely correct, and therefore steps must be taken within the contexts of general education classes and faculty advisement to help students who are not gifted intellectually to discern what their God-given attributes are and the best ways in which to develop them in order to enhance each individual's sense of being part of God's "elite." Every instructor employed by a Christian institution of higher learning should be equipped to give holistic guidance to each student who comes under his or her aegis. At the same time, the grade point average need not be the sole criteria for inclusion in an "honors" course. A designation such as "with permission of the instructor" would open the door for a teacher to allow other than intellectually gifted students to participate on a discretionary basis.

Students who have determined their major field of study or who aim at a specific career goal should be banded together in a close community of fellowship. They must be *carefully* and *individually* educated and trained, with each individual challenged to attain the *maximum* of his or her own potential. Finally, each must be endued with a sense of *mission*. The undisciplined children of the current generation must be equipped with a ruthless discipline in every area of life—spiritual, mental, moral and physical. They must be honed and sharpened until they become instruments of devastating effectiveness, motivated to exercise their knowledge and skills in whatever situations the course of life places them. As Paul reminds Timothy, the Christian revelation is designed to make us "thoroughly equipped for every good work" (2 Timothy 3:17).

We have observed that most young people today lack a sense of tradition or heritage. Consequently, studies in history must form a consistent part of their education. But in order to be meaningful, these studies must be of a *contextual* history, emphasizing aspects of the past which link directly to the mission that students are preparing for today.

A biblical view of history as a product of the sovereignty of God must form the foundation upon which all subsequent aspects of learning are built. Students who aim at the pastorate or the mission field must come to understand that they are participants in a cosmic "search and rescue" operation which was begun in Genesis 3 and which will not end until Revelation 20. In addition, the Bible must be taught as it was meant to be taught: from a missiological perspective. A hermeneutical system which gives preeminence to any theological topic other than missiology is a system which is essentially erroneous in its approach to the Word of

God. Our theology, Christology, pneumatology, soteriology, ecclesiology and eschatology must all be rooted in missiology; otherwise, they are hopelessly skewed.

5. *Generate programs which produce specific identity constructs.* The characteristics of biblical apostolicity (as seen in 1 Corinthians 9) and of biblical eldership and deaconship (as recorded in 1 Timothy 3:1-13) must become the core around which the curricula of Bible institutes, Bible colleges, Christian liberal arts institutions and seminaries are formed. Biblical apostolicity consists of the abilities to gather Christians into a definable church structure (1 Corinthians 9:1-2), to be a wise steward of finances (3-15), to preach the gospel with passion (16-18), to adapt oneself to various cultures, races, and social classes (19-23), and to exercise a ruthless self-discipline (24-27). The qualities characterizing an elder and deacon include an exemplary lifestyle, marital faithfulness, balance and control of self, hospitality, teaching ability, sobriety, gentleness, proper family relationships, mature and sound judgment, and the respect of non-Christians.

Each of these aspects must be clearly addressed in some way in *every* ministry-oriented course that a student takes. Furthermore, the *life principles, values and skills* which underlie all of these abilities or states must appear in "liberal arts" courses as well. Such principles, values and skills need not be overtly "biblical" (in the sense that chapter and verse must be cited at every turn), but the knowledge that one's students are required—biblically speaking—to be participants in ministry no matter what occupation or career they choose should shape the content of each philosophy, psychology, literature, science, history, mathematics, writing, music and physical education course that is offered.

But courses are not just taught—they are taught by *people*. Great care is necessary not only in the selection of our educational curricula but of our educators as well. The résumés of faculty members at these institutions should ideally reflect education and experience on both the "secular" and "sacred" sides of academia and culture in general. In recruiting professors in liberal arts fields, evangelical institutions should insist upon a significant amount of Christian education and/or ministry experience.

Conclusion

Those Christians who have chosen a life of service within Christian institutions of higher learning occupy a position of influence which has the potential of transforming the lives of literally millions of people.

The pastoral and missionary candidates that sit in the classrooms of these schools, along with those students who will influence the world through business, public school teaching, health care, counseling and other such professions will each contact dozens of persons in the course of their lives, who will in turn contact dozens of other persons, and so on.

Knowledge of the mechanics of exponential multiplication should cause the heart of every teacher to pound with excitement upon entering a classroom for any given lecture period. Such knowledge should also sober each instructor during his or her hours of preparation, knowing that errors or areas of neglect could be multiplied a thousandfold. No wonder James included in his letter the solemn warning that "not many of you should presume to be teachers, my brothers, because you know that we who teach will be judged more strictly" (3:1).

While this sober statement should remain constantly in the mind of every teacher, I prefer to dwell upon the more positive theme found in Acts 19, where Paul's two-year "Bible institute," housed in the lecture hall of Tyrannus, produced men and women who were so well-equipped and so fired with enthusiasm for mission that "all the Jews and Greeks who lived in the province of Asia heard the word of the Lord" (19:10). May such a saturation of entire geographical areas become the goal—and the product—of our educational institutions today.

Endnotes

[1]   Some may question the religiosity of Catholic institutions like those mentioned above. For an in-depth analysis of the spiritual state of these schools, see David J. O'Brien, *From the Heart of the American Church: Catholic Higher Education and American Culture* (Maryknoll, NY: Orbis Books, 1994). See also George Marsden, *The Outrageous Idea of Christian Scholarship* (New York: Oxford University Press, 1997), 101-104.

[2]   For a detailed examination of the transformation of Christian institutions, see George Marsden, *The Soul of the American University: From Protestant Establishment to Established Nonbelief* (New York: Oxford University Press, 1994), hereafter cited *SAU* and Mark Noll, *The Scandal of the Evangelical Mind* (Grand Rapids, MI: Eerdmans, 1994).

[3]   A great deal of A.B. Simpson's missionary motivation arose from his desire to "bring back the King" (see Robert Niklaus, et. al., *All for Jesus* [Camp Hill, PA: Christian Publications, 1986], 73). Hudson Taylor's philosophy of ministry was also a primary example of this type of thinking. Evangelism pure and simple was the goal of the China Inland Mission.

[4]   See H. Richard Niebuhr, *Christ and Culture* (New York: Harper, 1951).

[5]   College rankings are often based on surveys taken of various college presidents as to which institutions they would rank as the highest. Rankings are also based on such

items as "selectivity"—a concept which is essentially circular, in the sense that a school, for whatever reason, suddenly finds itself "popular" or "attractive" and is flooded with applications, which in turn increases its ability to be selective, which in turn establishes the school's reputation as "selective," which increases the number of applications from students (or the parents of students) who desire the prestige of a "selective" college, and so on. See Amy E. Graham and Robert J. Morse, "Our Method Explained," *U.S. News and World Report* (August 31, 1998): 82.

6   Marsden, *SAU*, 438.

7   James Davison Hunter, *Evangelicalism: The Coming Generation* (Chicago: The University of Chicago Press, 1987), 176-177. One notable flaw in Hunter's study is that when he speaks of "evangelical higher education" he does not include either Bible institutes or Bible colleges. Whether this omission is due to the fact that none of these institutions has ever come close to appearing in the rankings of, say, *U.S. News and World Report*'s annual college edition, or whether Hunter himself does not consider the academic process at these institutions to be worthy of the term "higher education" is not forthcoming. He does explain that "the limitations of time and expense prohibited their inclusion in the sample," but this is rather unconvincing. Washington Bible College, Philadelphia College of the Bible, Lancaster Bible College and even Columbia Bible College are all an easy drive from Charlottesville, Virginia.

8   According to research reported by the Council for Christian Colleges and Universities, the actual figure is forty-seven percent. See Christine J. Gardner, "Keeping Students in School," *Christianity Today* (September 7, 1998): 34.

9   See, for instance, Scott Bessenecker, "Paul's Short-term Church Planting: Can It Happen Again?" *Evangelical Missions Quarterly* (July 1997): 326ff.

10   Max Weber, *The Protestant Ethic and the Spirit of Capitalism* (New York: Charles Scribner's Sons, 1958).

11   The "double filtration" spoken of here involves first of all the filtration of those who dared to step onto a boat sailing across the Atlantic to begin with. Generally speaking, only the bravest, the hardiest, the most stubborn or the most desperate were willing to risk the dangers of ocean travel at that time. The second filtration occurred when those who arrived on the shores of America then found it necessary to survive in an undeveloped country. Those who were able to get through the winters were the bravest of the brave, the hardiest of the hardy, the most stubborn of the stubborn and the most desperate of the desperate. The result of this two-stage filtering has produced a pool of citizens unique in the world's history.

12   In his book *In Defense of Elitism*, William A. Henry III cites the work of Cornell University professor Donald Hayes, which reveals that prior to World War II, general eighth grade textbooks were of the same level of rigor as senior-level honors textbooks today. See William A. Henry III, *In Defense of Elitism* (New York: Anchor Books, 1994), 42.

13   See Christopher Lasch, *The Culture of Narcissism* (New York: W.W. Norton & Co., 1991), and Stephen Carter, *The Culture of Disbelief* (New York: Basic Books, 1993).

14   Richard Mouw notes this trend, along with some of its implications for evangelical higher education, in a chapter entitled "The Challenge of Evangelical Theological Education," in *Theological Education in the Evangelical Tradition*, ed. D.G. Hart and R. Albert Mohler, Jr. (Grand Rapids, MI: Baker Books, 1996), 287.

15 According to John 13:3, Jesus was able to wash the feet of His disciples because He knew who He was, where He had come from and where He was going. Those who do not possess such knowledge will be unable to serve effectively in any context.

16 For a very fine perspective on the conditions existing within today's student population, see Ken Baker, "Boomers, Busters, and Missions: Things Are Different Now," *Evangelical Missions Quarterly* (January 1997): 70ff.

17 Not only is such thinking futile; it also violates a clear biblical precept. Ecclesiastes 7:10 states: "Do not say, 'Why were the old days better than these?' For it is not wise to ask such questions."

18 It is ironic that the same Protestants who have railed against Roman Catholic conservatism with regard to the use of Latin in the Mass have for all practical intents and purposes created the same aura for Greek within Protestant circles. Greek should continue to be an option for students intending ministry. It should not, however, be required, but rather made one alternative among many.

19 For more on this subject, see Ken Dychtwald and Joe Flower, *The Age Wave* (New York: Bantam Books, 1990).

20 See the article by Rodney Clapp entitled "Remonking the Church" in *Christianity Today* (August 12, 1988), 20.

21 In 1977, Phil Parshall authored an article in the *Evangelical Missions Quarterly* which advocated limitation of family size by missionary couples to a maximum of two children. The article was well-reasoned and carefully balanced. The letters to the editor which appeared in future volumes, however, were in most cases passionate denunciations of the very idea, and were neither well-reasoned nor balanced. See Phil Parshall, "A Small Family Is a Happy Family," *Evangelical Missions Quarterly* (October 1977): 207ff.

22 For more on this issue, see Ruth A. Tucker, "Growing Up a World Away," *Christianity Today* (February 17, 1989), 17ff.

23 The 1997 edition of the *The Mission Handbook* notes that while the number of long-term missionaries increased by 1.3% between 1992 and 1996, the number of short-termers increased by 28.2%. And while in 1992 38,968 persons were involved in terms of service ranging from two weeks to one year, by 1996 that number had swelled to 63,995. See John Siewert and Edna Valdez, eds., *The Mission Handbook*, 17th edition (Pasadena, CA: MARC, 1997), 74.

24 See, for instance, Douglas Letson and Michael Higgens, *The Jesuit Mystique* (Chicago: Loyola Press, 1995).

About the Authors

Matthew Cook, Ph.D., is pastor of Faith Bible Church in Millersburg, OH. Beginning this summer he is a missionary appointee to West Africa.

Elio Cuccaro, Ph.D., is Professor of Theology and Ministry at Nyack College, Nyack, NY and Senior Editor at Christian Publications, Inc., Camp Hill, PA.

David Fessenden, BA, is Managing Editor of Christian Publications, Inc., the publishing house of The Christian and Missionary Alliance.

Richard Pease, D. Miss., is Head of the Department of Missiology and Religion at Nyack College, Nyack, NY.

Larry Poston, Ph.D., is Professor of Religion at Nyack College, Nyack, NY.

David John Smith, M.Div., is Senior Pastor of the Quinte Alliance Church in Belleville, Ontario, Canada.

Eldon Woodcock, Ph.D., is Professor of Bible at Nyack College, Nyack, NY.